D0773014

SH383.5C32P76Y93
BASQUE WHALING IN LABR
PROULX JEAN-PIER

Basque Whaling in Labrador in the 16th Century

Jean-Pierre Proulx

Translated from the Original French

Studies in Archaeology, Architecture and History

National Historic Sites
Parks Service
Environment Canada

Available in Canada through authorized bookstore agents and other bookstores, or by mail from the Canada Communication Group – Publishing, Supply and Services Canada, Ottawa, Ontario, Canada, K1A 0S9.

Published under the authority of the Minister of the Environment, Ottawa, 1993.
Editing: Sheila Ascroft
Design: Suzanne Adam-Filion
Production: Suzanne H. Rochette and Rod Won
Translation: Secretary of State

Parks publishes the results of its research in archaeology, architecture and history. A list of publications is available from National Historic Sites Publications, Parks Service, Environment Canada, 1600 Liverpool Court, Ottawa, Ontario, K1A 0H3.

Canadian Cataloguing in Publication Data

Proulx, Jean-Pierre, 1943-
Basque whaling in Labrador in the 16th century
(Studies in archaeology, architecture and history, ISSN 0821-1027)
Issued also in French under title: Les Basques et la pêche de la baleine au Labrador au XVIe siècle.
Includes bibliographical references.
ISBN 0-660-14819-6
DSS cat. no. R61-2/9-59E

1. Whaling — Newfoundland — Labrador — History — 16th century. 2. Whaling — Newfoundland — History — 16th century. 3. Labrador (Nfld.) — History. 4. Newfoundland — History — To 1763. I. Canadian Parks Service. National Historic Sites. II Title. III. Series.

SH383.5C32P76 1992 639.2'8'097182 C93-099411-6

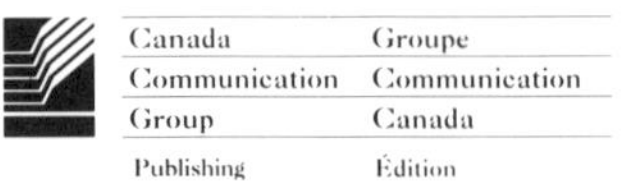

Table of Contents

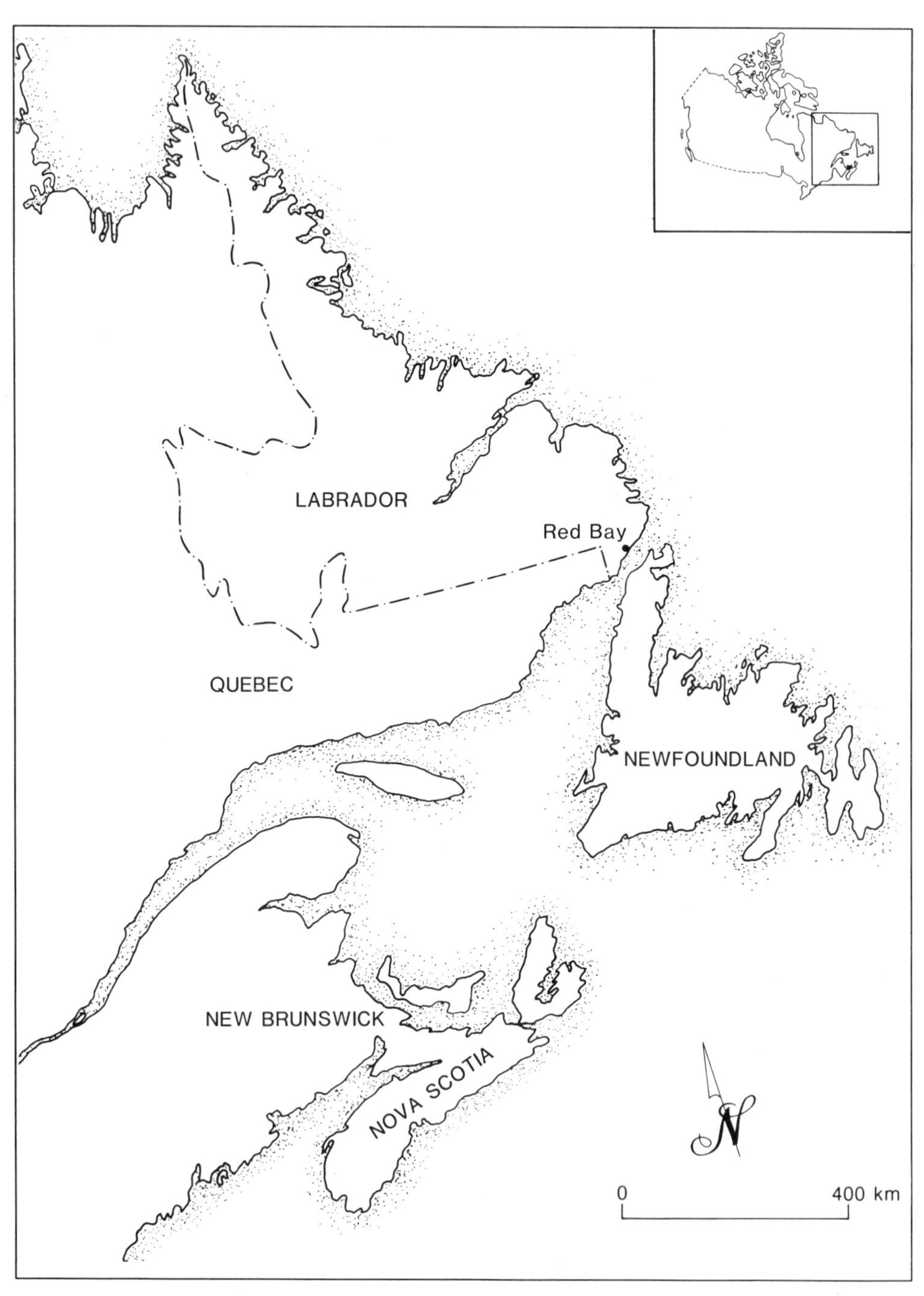

1. Red Bay, on the east coast of Canada. *Drawing : Dorothea Kappler.*

Introduction

Four hundred years ago, a Basque whaleman named Joanes de Echaniz dictated his last will as he lay in the forecastle of a ship anchored in a Labrador port. The very fact that this item of apparent trivia only recently came to light tells us a great deal about the gaps in certain periods of our history. Canadian historiography has almost completely overlooked a significant chapter in our country's history — the exploitation by Europeans of our East Coast fisheries in the second half of the 16th century. Most historians have concentrated on the official voyages of the explorers, from Cabot's in 1497 to the third voyage of Cartier in 1541. After this last voyage the historiography of Canada is almost silent until the founding of New France by Champlain at the beginning of the 17th century. And yet in the 60-year interval, Canada continued to attract Europeans in general and Basques in particular. No longer explorers sent on an official voyage by their King, the new arrivals were individual whalemen and fishermen who came to exploit the riches of Canadian waters off what is now Newfoundland and Labrador. It is far more difficult to document unofficial expeditions than official ones, because of the problems involved in obtaining records and the arduous and time-consuming work needed to collect and analyse them. As a result, many historians have been content to sum up this important half-century in a few lines.

Among the few studies that have attempted a thorough investigation of European whalers, especially Basques, in what are now Canadian waters is the brief yet thoughtful work of C.R. Markham in 1881.[1] After his promising start, Canadian

---

1 Sir Clements R. Markham, "On the Whale-Fisheries of the Basque Provinces of Spain," *Nature*, Vol. 25 (1882), pp. 365-68.

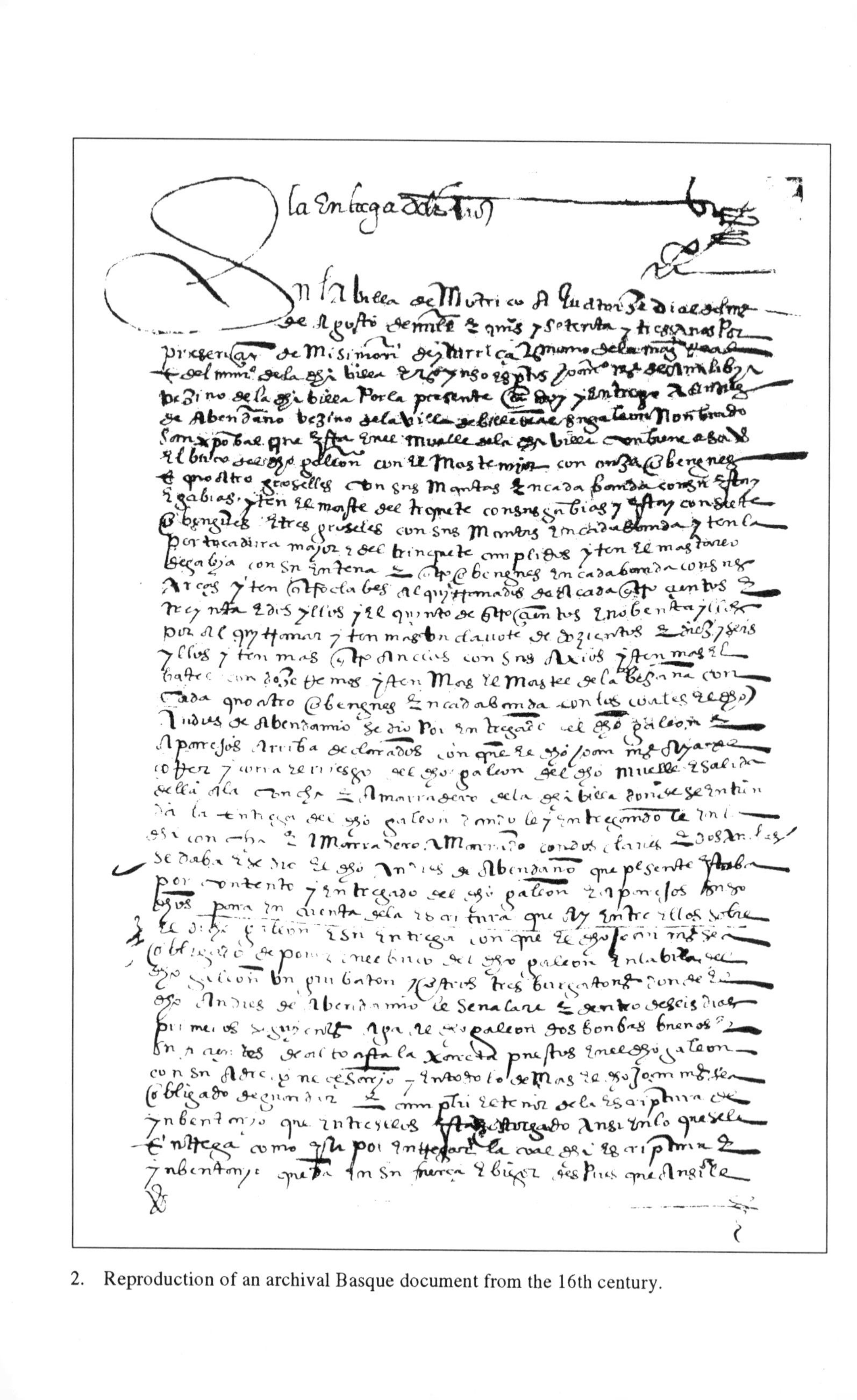

2. Reproduction of an archival Basque document from the 16th century.

historiography would have to wait another half-century for Harold Innis to attempt — with somewhat mixed results — to broaden our knowledge of this period.[2] He would be followed by other North American historians who, without necessarily devoting all their energy to the systematic, intensive study of Basque whalemen, nevertheless shed light on their presence along our coastline in the latter half of the 16th century.[3] In general, however, all the articles other than Markham's suffer from the same weakness of an inadequate quantity of documentary sources; in addition, the information-gathering methods used are dubious. For example, all of Innis's conclusions are based on the Vargas Ponce collection. Despite its intrinsic interest, this collection mostly consists of transcripts of official documents such as briefs, reports, claims, and decrees. And not only are there few of these documents, but they are frequently biased, since they are obviously intended to support a case. Based on this type of information, Innis occasionally came to erroneous conclusions or made false assumptions, which were often blindly adopted by other historians.

In fact, it is only recently that researchers have taken an interest in the abundant unofficial records of the second half of the 16th century found in the departmental and provincial archives of France and Spain.[4] These collections, which consist primarily of insurance policies, trial proceedings and notarial deeds, are an unexpected treasure trove that has made it possible for the first time to reconstruct our history during this period with some degree of accuracy. The texts contain amazing revelations about trading along the Atlantic coast at the time. For example, it has been discovered that whaling and fishing attracted more Europeans and as many ships as the famed Spanish *carrera de las Indias*, the spectacular fleets that ran to and from the West Indies. Cod was the most important species taken but research has shown that whales were hunted as well, a fact that had gone almost unmentioned in Canadian historiography. There is also a wealth of detail concerning the physical and social organization of the expeditions as well as the daily routines of the crews. From the

2 H.A. Innis, "The Rise and Fall of the Spanish Fishery in Newfoundland," *Proceedings and Transactions of the Royal Society of Canada*, 3rd. Series, Vol. 25, Section 11 (1931), pp. 51-70.

3 David B. Quinn, *North American Discovery: circa 1000-1612* (New York: Harper and Row, 1971); John Gilchrist, "Exploration and Enterprise: the Newfoundland Fishery, ca. 1497-1677," in *Canadian Business History* (Toronto: MacMillan, 1972); Gillian T. Cell, *English Enterprise in Newfoundland, 1577-1660* (Toronto: University Press, 1969).

4 In particular, Selma Barkham and her son Michael for Spain, and Laurier Turgeon for France (see bibliography).

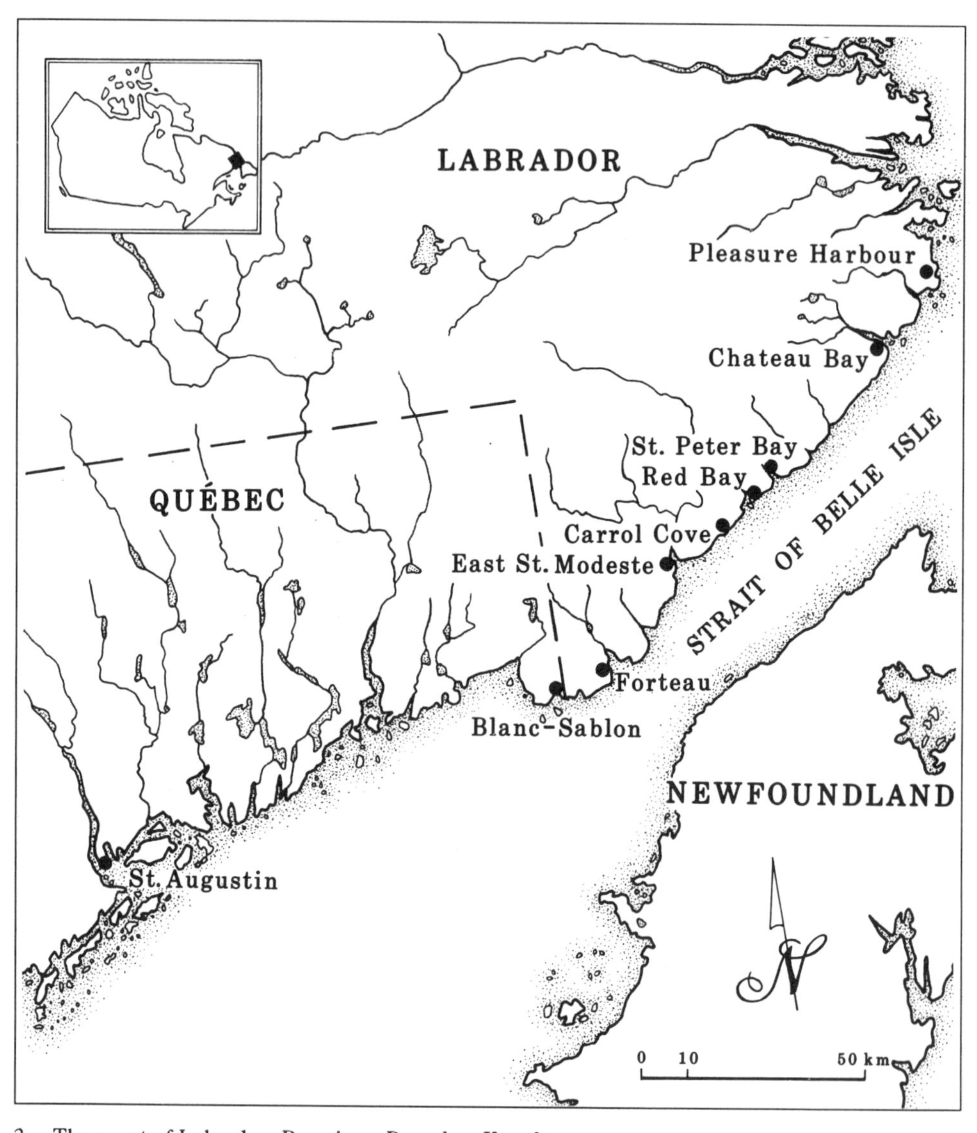

3. The coast of Labrador. *Drawing : Dorothea Kappler.*

legal documents in particular we now know about provisioning, clothing, customs, hunting techniques, etc. We know enough to reconstruct a whaling expedition to the Labrador coast, from the time of getting ready to set sail right to the point of mooring at home port after the voyage.

In reading these wonderful documents, Selma Barkham discovered information about a Basque whaler that had gone down off the port of Buytres in 1565. She found an insurance claim by two harpooners for recovery of a number of barrels of whale oil that had been saved by Joanes de Portu from the wreck of a ship owned by Ramos de Arrieta, known as Borda. From other documents, Barkham was able to identify the ship as the San Juan. In a paper read to the Society for Historical Archaeology in 1976, Barkham linked the geographical name of Buytres with the port of Red Bay, Labrador. Intrigued by the mystery, and by the adventure of learning more about the geography of the area, Barkham went on her own voyage of discovery to Labrador in 1977. She was accompanied by her son Michael, archaeologist Graham Rowley, Walter Kenyon of the Royal Ontario Museum, and James Tuck of Memorial University, St John's, Nfld. After seeing the region for herself, Barkham was able to make the connection between several of the place-names mentioned in the documents and ports in Labrador. In addition to Buytres, which she had previously identified as Red Bay, Puerto Nuevo became Pleasure Harbour, Chateo was Chateau Bay, and Los Hornos was East St. Modeste.[5] All down the coastline, the scientists found evidence that the Basques had been in the region. Red roof tiles, foundations of the "ovens" used for trying (boiling down) whale blubber into oil, and shards of pottery were discovered in all the ports that she had identified from the documents as 16th-century whaling stations. Michael Barkham also discovered a harpoon head dating from that period.

Selma Barkham related her discoveries to Robert Grenier, the head of marine archaeology unit of the Canadian Parks Service, and suggested that he send a diving expedition to Red Bay, which is opposite the northern tip of Newfoundland about 100 km northeast of Blanc Sablon. The expedition set off in early September 1978. Grenier and three of his staff dove a few times and came back up with a piece of oak. According to the records, oak was the Basque shipbuilders' choice of wood, and oak is not a native species on the Labrador coast. The divers cleaned off some of the silt deposit from the ocean floor — and found themselves in the presence of a wreck that

---

5 Among recently discovered names of ports, one noteworthy example is Canada Pequeña, which probably corresponds to St. Augustin.

had all the characteristics of a 16th-century ship! It was most likely the *San Juan*, mentioned in the documents discovered by Barkham. The wreck was found 10 metres down, off to the north of Saddle Island, opposite the trenches excavated the previous summer by James Tuck's team of archaeologists. When the ship sank, the masts and poop must have been visible above the waterline, but ice, wind and waves would have made short work of them, so that by 1978 nothing remained of the ship but its hull. The wreck was resting on its keel, the two sides having foundered along either side of the centre-line, like an open book. Most parts had been extraordinarily well preserved by the icy waters of the Strait of Belle Isle and the protective layer of silt. The wood was perfectly sound and it was still easy to identify the species. Even the marks of tools and wear were still visible. However, the salt water had completely rusted out all the metal artifacts, except for a swivel-gun and an anchor.

The discovery of the wreck was a first, not just in Canada but anywhere. Except for the remains of another ship, off the southern tip of Florida, the wreck of the *San Juan* was and still is the oldest ever found in North America. At the same time, the heritage of Canada was enriched by the beautifully preserved and intact remains of a 16th-century ship and of the oldest whale-blubber processing works in the world. In 1979, the Historic Sites and Monuments Board of Canada recognized the distinctiveness of this find by designating the Red Bay area as a place of national historic significance.

This decision was to lead to the development and implementation of an extensive program of research concerning the Basque whaling industry. The program involved the conservation, historical research and marine archaeological divisions of the Canadian Parks Service and brought in the anthropology and geology departments of Memorial University, the Zooarchaeological Identification Centre of the National Museums' Canadian Conservation Institute, the National Archives of Canada, the Government of Newfoundland, the Canadian Social Sciences and Humanities Research Council, the Canadian Forestry Service and the Department of Fisheries and Oceans. This publication is the fruit of the research conducted principally by the Historical Research Division of the Canadian Parks Service.[6]

---

6 Also see: Jean-Pierre Proulx, *Whaling in the North Atlantic From Earliest Times to the Mid-19th Century* (Ottawa: Parks Canada, 1986). This is an introduction to the present study, which describes the Basque whaling industry off Labrador in detail. Based exclusively on documentary sources, *Whaling in the North Atlantic* is divided into five chapters. The first surveys whaling from prehistoric times until the 11th century, while the other four chapters deal with Basque, English, Dutch, and American whaling activities.

Chapter I
The Basques in Labrador in the 16th Century

Since so many documents have burned or disappeared from the municipal archives of Bordeaux, Bayonne, Pau, Saint-Jean-de-Luz and San Sebastián [Donostia][1] and because such major depositories as those of Bordeaux, Tolosa, Oñate [Oñati] and Bilbao have not yet been fully explored, it is impossible to determine precisely when the Basques first went whale-hunting. In Spain, the oldest known record that provides reliable evidence of whaling is the 14th-century *fuero* or grant of rights of the town of San Sebastián. In France, the rent-roll of Bayonne cathedral is the first documentary evidence, and it is a hundred years older than the *fuero*. Actually, it would not be unreasonable to suggest that the origins of the Basque whale-hunt go back even farther, to the 7th century, when the Basques were sending oil to Jumièges to light the local monastery.[2]

Whenever they actually began hunting whale, the Basques mastered this art very quickly, moving ahead of all their North European competitors. The decline of the whale hunt in Northern Europe coincided with the peak of Basque whaling activity in the 13th and 14th centuries. At that time, the hunt was carried on along the coast, providing significant revenues throughout the Basque country, from Bayonne to Bilbao.

---

1 The Basque names are given in square brackets

2 Jean-Pierre Proulx, *op. cit.*, p. 15

This type of whale hunting seems to have gradually disappeared from the Bay of Biscay beginning in the 15th century. For some reason not yet understood, the Basque hunters moved out into the Atlantic at that time. The most generally accepted theory is that intensive hunting between the 12th and 15th centuries had made whales scarce in the waters off the Basque country. There is as yet no satisfactory proof of this view, and it would appear unlikely, given the techniques then in use. Even if the catch along the Basque coast did decrease in the 15th century, this could not possibly have been because of overhunting.[3] In comparison to the modern-day hunt Basque catches were insignificant. Parish records show that the Basques would never have caught more than 100 whales in a season.[4] The English, Dutch and American whalers who took over the whaling scene in the 17th century caught many times more whales than the Basques caught up to the 15th century, and yet it took them over a century to reduce stocks of sperm whales and right whales to the point where expeditions became unproductive and the species' survival was threatened.[5]

There are more plausible explanations for the Basques abandoning coastal whaling in the 15th century than the supposed disappearance of whales from the Bay of Biscay.

A change in the currents may have led to climatic changes in the Bay, forcing the whale to seek a more suitable habitat. While there is no hard evidence in support of this theory, there are examples in the case of other European marine species at this same time. Cod had at one time been abundant along the coasts of Spain, but moved westward toward the end of the Middle Ages, and according to the chronicles, herring deserted the Baltic in 1473.[6] The same could have happened to the Biscayne

---

3 "La equivocada idea que sobre la desaparición de los balénidos en nuestras costas oceánicas hace larga fecha se viene propalando por los naturalistas y balleneros, atribuyendo la causa sin gran fundamento a la persecución activa que los pescadores bascos, en siglos pasados, hicieron a los grandes cetáceos, que segun se dice, tanto abundaban en el mar Cantábrico." (The argument on the matter of the disappearance of whales in the waters of the Gulf of Biscay, where they were in abundance, comes from the naturalists and the whalemen who, without foundation, attribute the cause to intensive fishing of the great whales by Basque fishermen hundreds of years ago.) Jaime de Labayru y Goicoechea, *Historia general del Senorio de Vizcaya.* (Bilbao: La Gran Enciclopedia Vasca, 1899-1920), Vol. 1, p. 594, note 1.

4 Ivan T. Sanderson, *Follow the Whale* (Boston: Little, Brown & Co., 1956), p. 130.

5 It is possible that the number of right whales was less than that of other species, but no statistics are available to back this up.

6 Fernand Braudel, *Civilisation matérielle et capitalisme; XVe-XVIIIe siècles* (Paris: Armand Colin, 1967), p. 162.

right whale, forcing the hunters to follow it. The plausibility of this theory, however, is somewhat diminished by the fact that a minority of whalers continued to hunt along the Basque shore even after the 15th century.[7]

It is also understandable that after being hunted for three centuries along the shores of the Bay, the whales would instinctively have moved away from the dangerous area. Whales are known to have a highly developed instinct. The Biscayne whale may have continued to live in the Bay over the winter, but most of them may have stayed away from the shore, obliging the hunters to follow them out onto the high seas. This phenomenon would not be unique in the history of whaling; it was to occur in Spitsbergen in the 17th century.

But the likeliest possibility is that, encouraged by their success during the winter along the coasts of France and Spain, the Basques set off to find out where the whales congregated so they could hunt them all year around. This was the view expressed by Étienne Cleirac, a jurist and lawyer in Bordeaux, in his *Us et Coutumes de la Mer*:

> *The great profits, and the facility with which the inhabitants of Capbreton near Bayonne and the Basques of Aquitaine were able to catch the whales, were lures that made them bold enough to pursue their quest out onto the Ocean, to every latitude and longitude.*[8]

Whether because of a shortage of whales caused by excessive hunting or because they wanted to increase their income through year-round whaling, by the 15th century (perhaps earlier) the Basques had begun to move up the Atlantic coastline of Europe in search of their quarry. The move northward is additional evidence in favour of the view that they left the Bay of Biscay because they wanted to hunt whale all year long rather than sit and wait for the whales to come to them. The whales are known to have frequented the more northern waters before moving down to the Bay of Biscay in the autumn. The Basques apparently decided to extend the hunting season but still stay near their markets in northern Europe.

---

7 René Cuzacq, *Les Basques chasseurs de baleines* (Bayonne: published by author, 1972), pp. 34, 40 and 41. The Spanish documents also mention expeditions off Galicia, such as the voyage of the *Catalina* in 1544. The Basque Country, Archivo general de la disputacion de Guipuzcoa (AGDG). Tolosa. Corregimiento, Ejecutivos Mandiola, Legajo 13.

8 Étienne Cleirac, *Us et Coutumes de la Mer*, (Rouen: Jean Lucas, 1671), p. 129.

The dates and destinations of their expeditions are not certain. Some writers claim that the Basques reached Scotland in the 14th century[9] and Iceland in the year 1412.[10] Once in Iceland, it was only a step to America for these excellent navigators.

There can be no doubt that the Basques did indeed come to North America. The tombstones at Placentia in Newfoundland and the trying ovens on Île aux Basques, on the Mingan Islands in the St. Lawrence, and in Labrador are evidence that the Basques were here at a certain point in our history. What is not so certain, and much debated, is *when* they came. Some sources contend that the Basques discovered the New World long before Columbus.[11] This view is not implausible, for long before the famed explorer, Basque and Portuguese mariners were venturing far out to sea and if a crew lost its bearings and the craft were at the mercy of wind and tide, it might well have sailed very near America, perhaps actually skirting the coastline. But it is strange that no claim was made in the Basque popular tradition of the 16th and 17th centuries to have discovered America before Columbus.[12] Quite the reverse: the tradition flatly denies any such claim. In his seminal *Colección de los viajes y descubrimientos que hicieron por mar los españoles*, Martin Fernandez de Navarette mentions a contract dated 1511. It was between His Most Catholic Majesty Ferdinand and the explorer Jean de Agramonte de Lerida, who agrees to take two ships, outfitted at his own expense, to learn the secrets of the New Found Land. The crews were to be engaged locally, except for two pilots from Brittany or any other nation that had already gone to those parts.[13] This suggests there may have been no Basque pilot familiar with the region to be explored.

As well, Jean de la Cosa, who had been with Columbus in 1492 and was fully abreast of the nautical discoveries of his era and the traditions concerning the discovery of the New Land, attributes the discovery to the English, alluding no doubt to

9 J.B. Bailac, *Nouvelle chronique de la ville de Bayonne* (Bayonne: Duhart-Fauvet, 1827), p. 57.

10 Mario Ruspoli, *À la recherche du cachalot* (Paris: Éditions de Paris, 1955), p. 66.

11 See the papers quoted in Jacques Heers, *Christophe Colomb* (Paris: Hachette, 1981), p. 168; Maxime Dégros, "La grande pêche basque des origines à la fin du XVIIIe siècle," *Bulletin de la Société des Sciences, Arts et Lettres de Bayonne*, No. 35 (1940), p. 167; Paul Courteault, *Pour l'histoire de Bordeaux et du Sud-Ouest* (Paris: Auguste Picard, 1914), p. 177; Ramon Seoane y Ferrer, *Los marinos Guipuzcoanos* (Madrid: Revista general de marina, 1908), p. 19; Édouard Ducéré, *Les pêcheurs basques à Terre-Neuve* (no place: no publisher, no date), p. 250, note 1.

12 Mariano Ciriquiain Gaiztarro, *Los Vascos en la pesca de la ballena* (San Sebastián: Ediciones Vascas, 1961), pp. 182-87.

13 Quoted in Édouard Ducéré, *op. cit.*, p. 251.

the voyage of John Cabot.[14] It is true that, unlike other peoples, the Basques seem not to have engaged in the practice of officially claiming possession of lands they visited in the course of their expeditions. In that era, exploration was sponsored by the government, but fishing and hunting were individual pursuits. The Basques were neither explorers nor colonizers. They were hunters who wanted to keep their routes secret and were thus very reticent about writing down anything that might make it easier for their competitors.

One thing that is certain is that before 1493 no map or document or story with the exception of the Viking sagas mentions America in any definite and unmistakable way. Because 15th-century cartographic and toponymic practices were imprecise, it is not certain that the lands indicated on pre-Columbian maps really were America. Before the appearance of the portolano in the 13th century, maps were not navigational aids but simply graphic representations of medieval accounts containing details both real and imagined. Depictions of these far-off isles might even have been the result of the Viking discoveries of 400 years earlier, preserved in oral tradition.

The first irrefutable evidence of a Basque presence in America dates from the first half of the 16th century. The vast schools of cod that Cabot had found in 1497 are probably what drew the Basques to our shores.[15] The first to outfit expeditions to the New Land were the northern Basques — those living under the French king — and the first indisputable reference to such expeditions dates from 1517.[16] Beginning in 1520, records from Bayonne contain references to cod-fishing expeditions to "Terrenabes," including one mention of a privateer from Saint-Jean-de-Luz in 1528.[17] The archives of La Rochelle mention 65 expeditions to the New Land from 1523 to

---

14 *Ibid.*, p. 253.

15 In a lawsuit between the abbot of Fécamp and a ship outfitter from Selles, the outfitter claimed that in 1487, Harfleur was the port "auquel tous les navyres faisant la pesche des morues aux terres neufves arrivoient" (at which all ships that fished for cod in the new lands would dock). Éric Dardel, *État des pêches maritimes sur les côtes occidentales de la France au début du XVIIIe siècle. D'après les procès-verbaux de visite de l'Inspecteur des Pêches Le Masson du Parc, 1723-1732* (Paris: André Tournon, 1941), p. 107.

16 Laurier Turgeon, "Pêches basques en Atlantique Nord: XVIIe - XVIIIe siècle," PhD thesis, Centre d'Études canadiennes de Bordeaux, 1982, p. 10. Maxime Dégros mentions a document from the municipal archives of Capbreton, in which a Bayonne ship's captain refers to the "pesque a les Terres Nabes" (fishing in the new lands) as something that had been quite common since 1512. Maxime Dégros, *op. cit.*, No. 35 (1940), p. 166. According to Turgeon, there is nothing of the sort in these archives.

17 Édouard Ducéré, "Recherches historiques sur les corsaires de Saint-Jean-de-Luz" in *La tradition au Pays Basque* (Donostia: Elkar, 1982), p. 219

1550, while the archives of Bordeaux contain over 100 such references for the period between 1517 and 1550.[18] Many of these voyages were led by northern Basques, who in 1545 accounted for almost 50 percent of La Rochelle's trade with the New Land and 75 percent of the Bordeaux trade.[19]

The northern Basques may have been well ensconced in the fishery off the New Land in the first half of the 16th century; the southern Basques, those living under the Spanish crown, were not. Various accounts suggest that the southern Basques did not go to Terranova (as the Spanish called it) on a regular basis or in large numbers before the 1540s. This is the view of the historian Navarette, who analysed a 1561 inquiry into the two percent tithe exacted by a religious order and two churches in San Sebastián on the income from the Terranova fishery. A 70-year-old witness reported that the fishery had only been active for the previous 17 to 20 years.[20] This statement is corroborated in 1576 by the deposition of Joannes de Echaçarreta of San Sebastián, who said that the fishery off the coast of Terranova dated back to around 1543.[21]

The archives of Tolosa also have records of a trial that refer to an expedition to Terranova in 1539 or 1540.[22] C. Fernandez Duro quotes a 1619 account in which the son of Matias de Echevete relates that in 1545 his father, then 15 years of age, was the first southern Basque to sail to Terranova on a ship from Ciboure [Ziburu] outfitted for cod-fishing.[23] On his return, Echevete is said to have spread the news of his discovery and it was only upon learning of it that some southern Basques decided to engage in the trade for themselves. But we have only Echevete's own word for this claim, which is contradicted by earlier documents from the southern part of the Basque country. There are chronicles of voyages to Terranova by sailors from Orio

18 Paul Courteault, *op. cit.*, p. 182 and Jacques Bernard, *Navires et gens de mer de Bordeaux, 1400-1550* (Paris: S.E.V.P.E.N., 1968), p. 807. These counts must be on the conservative side because only some of the expeditions were registered with notaries.

19 Laurier Turgeon, "Pêcheurs basques et Indiens des côtes du Québec au XVIe siècle," paper read to the *Colloque franco-québécois d'histoire rurale comparée* held July 5-8, 1982 at Rochefort, p. 2.

20 Quoted in Henry Harrisse, *Découverte et évolution cartographique de Terre-Neuve* (Paris: Welter, 1900), p. LIX.

21 Selma Barkham, "Documentary Evidence for 16th Century Basque Whaling Ships in the Strait of Belle Isle" in *Early European Settlement and Exploitation in Atlantic Canada* (St. John's, Nfld.: Memorial University, 1982), p. 53.

22 The Basque Country. AGDG. Tolosa. Corregimiento, Civiles Mandiola, Legajo 77, fol. 21r. The document does not specify whether this was one of the first expeditions.

23 Édouard Ducéré, *Les pêcheurs..., op. cit.*, p. 253.

in 1530 and from San Sebastián in 1526.[24] And men from Lequeitio [Lekeitio] apparently frequented the island of Newfoundland starting in 1535.[25]

However, a plausible explanation is that the southern Basques were not particularly interested at first in intensive fishing off Terranova, although they must have known about the cod banks as a result of the 1525 expedition of Esteban Gomez, a Portuguese pilot in the service of Spain. The southern Basques may have been catching enough cod off Flanders, England and Ireland. Or perhaps Terranova cod was not of much interest to them before the mid-16th century: – in 1525, the cosmographer Diego Rivero wrote that so far the most valuable thing discovered around the island was cod, which was of little value.[26]

While the southern Basques do not seem to have been very interested in going after cod, whaling was familiar to them and highly prized by them. The Basque whalemen presumably learned from French cod-fishermen that there were whales in the waters around the New Land.

After 1545 the whale trade triggered a spectacular growth in the Basque economy, which followed the course of the European economic conjuncture up to the beginning of the 17th century.[27] In the 1550s, historical annals prove beyond a doubt that the ports of Pasajes [Pasaia], Renteria [Errenteria] and San Sebastián were outfitting many ships every year for whale hunting off Terranova and even up the St. Lawrence River. In his work of around 1550, *Le Grand Insulaire et Pilotage*, the cosmographer André Thévet wrote about an island near Thadoyzeau or Tadoussac where men came from Bayonne and Spain every year to hunt whale.[28]

---

24 Rafael Gonzalez Echegaray, *Balleneros Cántabros* (Santander: Institucion cultural de Cantábria, 1978), p. 55.

25 J.M. Ugartechea y Salinas, "La pesca tradicional en Lequeitio," *Anuario de Eusko-Folklore*, Vol. 22 (1967-68), p. 11.

26 "Hasta ahora, no se ha hallado cosa de provecho mas que los bacallaos que son de poca estima." (Up to now, we have found nothing of value except cod which is of little interest.) Ramon Seoane y Ferrer, *op. cit.*, p. 16. A few years later, Francis Bacon would state that cod was worth more than the mines of Peru!

27 Laurier Turgeon, "Pêcheurs basques...," *op. cit.*, p. 2.

28 In the early 16th century, the French name "Terreneuve" and the "English New Found Land" (also referred to here as New Land and Terranova) covered a much wider geographical area than modern-day Newfoundland. The expression had a very general meaning: "Il est tout certain et notoire que mariniers vont [...] es terres neufves [...]. En terre neufve a de bons ports et hables, Meilleurs deurope et fort belles rivieres, Grant pescherie... ." (It is an established and well-known fact that sailors go ... to the new lands.... In the new land there are good ports, better than in Europe, and fine rivers, great fishing banks....) René Bélanger, *Les Basques dans l'estuaire du Saint-Laurent 1535-1635*, (Montréal: Presses de l'Université du Québec, 1971), p. 36.

Whaling was regulated even in those early years, for in 1553, the Junta Particular [council] of Guipuzcoa petitioned the King to protest two decrees prohibiting captains from setting sail from the province without a permit from Don Luis Carvajal, the captain-general of the fleet.[29] The decree was rescinded but on April 21, 1557, Philip II proclaimed a new one that forbade any Spanish ships from going to Terranova without his permission, on the pretext that he was afraid they might be attacked by the French, with whom Spain was at war.[30]

Philip, however, really had in mind keeping the whaling ships and crews in the service of the Spanish Crown. We know that whalers protested this decree, because three months later, on July 15, the King granted permission to the people of Guipuzcoa, Biscaya and Cuatro Villas de la Mar to sail to Terranova, as long as their ships were armed.[31]

The peace treaty between France and Spain, signed at Cateau-Cambrésis in 1559 and sealed by the marriage of Philip II and Elizabeth of Valois, was a factor in the growing number of ships that went whaling in the 1560s. The truce put an end to the many fratricidal skirmishes and acts of piracy. On February 8, 1564, the southern and northern Basques even agreed on a mutual assistance pact.[32] The North American fisheries commanded as many ships as the whole of the Spanish-American trade, and more sailors.[33] In 1571, there were nearly 100 ships in the Basque fleet, of which 25 to 30 were whaling ships representing a total of 15,600 tons and employing nearly 4000 fishermen.[34] A few years later, Anthony Parkhurst, a merchant of Bristol who made his fourth voyage to the New Land in 1578, wrote that while there he had seen about 350 European ships fishing cod and another 30 to 40 engaged in the whale hunt.[35]

---

29 Spain. Madrid. Museo Naval. Coll. Vargas Ponce, Vol. 3, fol. 7.

30 Henry Harrisse, *op. cit.*, p. LX.

31 Spain. Madrid. Museo Naval, Vargas Ponce, Vol. 3, fol. 12.

32 *Ibid.*, Vol. 3, fol. 19.

33 Pierre Chaunu has estimated that the Spanish-American fleet consisted of between 50 and 100 ships of approximately 16,000 *toneladas*. In Laurier Turgeon, "Pêcheurs basques...," *op. cit.*, p. 2. Moreover, research has revealed 231 contracts related to the Terranova run for 1563 alone, and these are just the ones witnessed by the notary Brigot of Bordeaux. Jacques Bernard, *op. cit.*, p. 807, note 16.

34 Laurier Turgeon, "Pêcheurs basques...," *op. cit.*, p. 8, note 11. The provinces of Guipuzcoa and Biscaya alone had 85 ships of 100 or more *toneles*. Spain. Simancas. Archivo General de Simancas (AGS), Guerra Antigua, legajo 75-13.

35 Richard Hakluyt, *The Principal Navigations, Voyages, Traffiques & Discoveries of the English Nation...* (Glasgow: J. MacLehose & Sons, 1903), Vol. 3, pp. 10-11. Hérubel obviously misread the text because he maintains that 130 Basque ships were hunting for whale. Marcel A. Hérubel, "Baleines et baleiniers: étude d'économie maritime," *La Revue Maritime*, (May 1930), p. 609.

The whale hunt took place in the Gulf of St Lawrence, particularly around Labrador, since the whales had to swim along the Labrador coast when passing through the Strait of Belle Isle. Two species of right whale frequented these waters at the time: the Greenland (or bowhead) whale and the North Atlantic right whale (or Biscayne whale). These species move relatively slowly; more importantly, they float after death, so they were ideal quarry for the Basques. They also produce oil and baleen in quantity, particularly the Greenland whale. This species now lives much farther north, but archaelogical excavation has revealed that in the 16th century it comprised two-thirds of the total Labrador whale catch. In the Muscovy Company's nomenclature for Spitsbergen whales, completed in the early 17th century, this species is referred to as the Grand Bay Whale, Grand Bay being the name the Basques had given to their Labrador whaling ground some years earlier. The Biscayne right whale is now very rarely seen around Newfoundland.

The earliest reference to a whaling industry in Labrador is 1547. Martin de Licona outfitted his ship the *Madalena*, for a whale and cod-fishing voyage which would take place the following year.[36] In 1554, four ships including the *Barbara* and the *Maria* from Orio, were seized in the port of Los Hornos or present-day East St. Modeste by northern Basques, who took them to Butus (Red Bay).[37] A few years later, the ports of Blanc Sablon, East St. Modeste, Red Bay, St. Peter Bay, Chateau Bay and Carrol Cove were buzzing with activity from June to late autumn. About twenty southern Basque ships hunted whale in this area every year in the 1570s, employing 1500 to 2000 men, and Red Bay was the station used by more than half of them.[38] The Basque archives list the names of 175 captains and officers who came to the Strait of Belle Isle before 1580.[39] By 1565, the original name "las partes de Terra Nueva" had been replaced by "la provincia de Terranova." This change (from "parts" to "province") suggests that the Basques had already established dominion over this region barely 20 years after their first expeditions.[40]

---

36 Selma Barkham, op. cit., p. 55.

37 Selma Barkham, "The Spanish Province of Terranova," unpublished, 1974, p. 2.

38 Michael Barkham, *Aspects of Life aboard Spanish Basque Ships during the 16th Century, with Special Reference to Terranova Whaling Voyages* (Ottawa: Parks Canada, 1981), p. 34.

39 F. Jose I. Lasa, "Reales cedulas sobre las pesquerias de Terranova," *Aranzazu*, Vol. 57, Nos. 581 and 582, p. 23.

40 The Basque Country. AGDG. Tolosa. Corregimiento, Civiles Elorza, Vol. 65, fol. 32r.

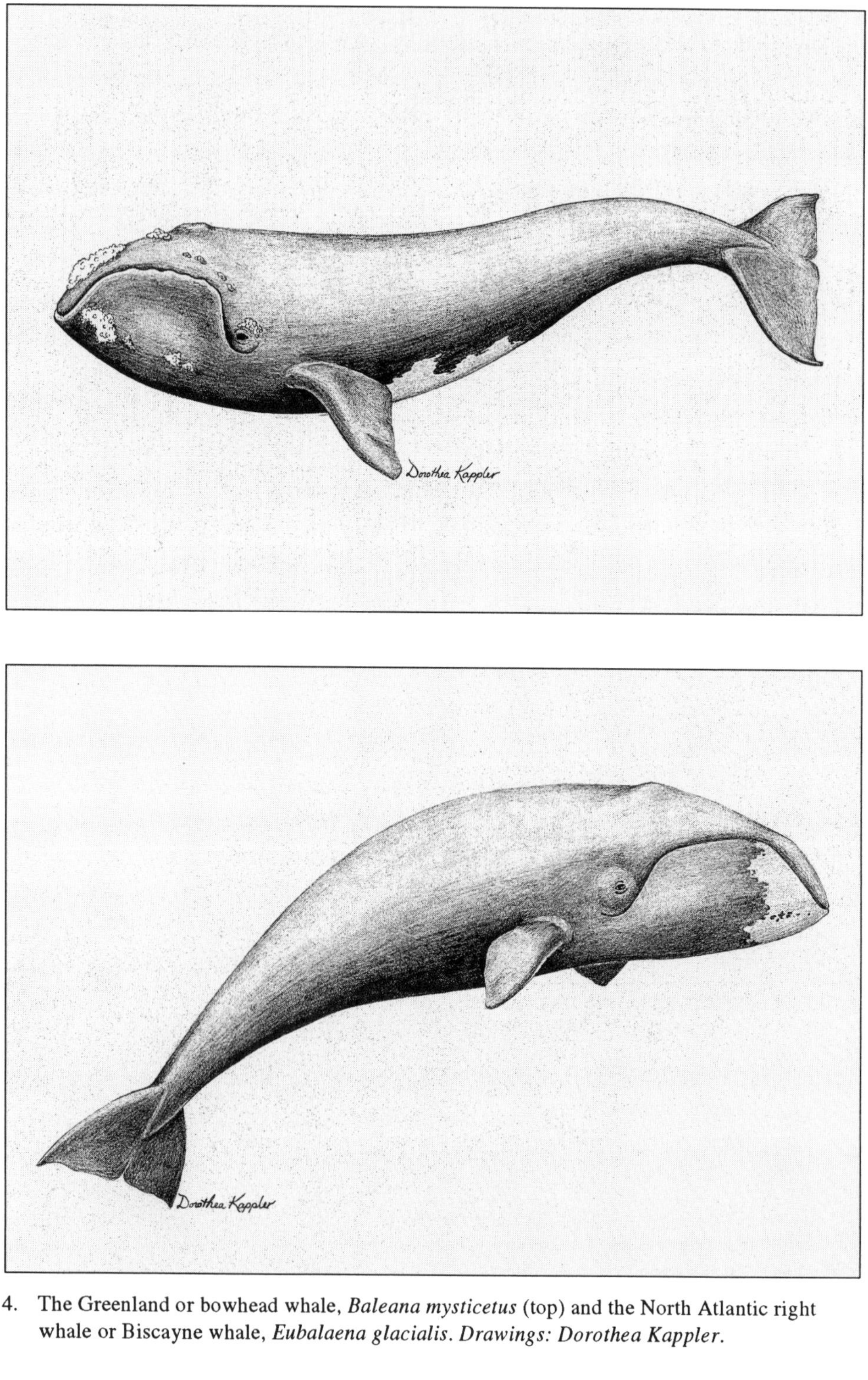

4. The Greenland or bowhead whale, *Baleana mysticetus* (top) and the North Atlantic right whale or Biscayne whale, *Eubalaena glacialis*. *Drawings: Dorothea Kappler.*

Red Bay seems to have been the whalers' favourite of all the Labrador ports. Well-known since the first days of whaling in the Gulf, it attracted a disproportionate share of whalemen every year. In 1575, as many as 11 whalers came to stay in Red Bay.[41] According to a statement by Juan de Echevete in 1619, 540 people died there in the winter of 1577.[42] The 125 human skeletons found by archaeologists between 1978 and 1982 are perhaps related to this disaster, as may be the second-oldest recorded will in Canadian history, written at Red Bay on June 22, 1557 by Juan Martinez de Larrume.[43] In 1579, the cartographer and pilot Martin Hoyarsabal named the bay Boytus.[44] Red Bay is described as follows by Augustin Le Gardeur de Tilly, sieur de Courtemanche, in 1705:

> *It was also in this harbour that the whales were once hunted. According to the Savages, the Eskimos made the Europeans leave. One can still see the ovens where the oil was made, and the bones of the whales which lie on the shore like overturned tree trunks one atop the other. They must have killed more than two or three thousand, to judge from the quantity of bones which we counted: 90 heads in just one place, of enormous size.*[45]

It is also in the port of Red Bay that a Basque ship, the *San Juan*, was reported to have sunk in 1565. The galleon belonged to one Ramos de Arrieta, known as Borda, from Pasajes. It could carry at least 1000 barrels of whale oil and a crew of about 75. The *San Juan* was a 25-ton ship — a respectable size for the mid-16th century. Not being securely anchored, it apparently went down in a storm as the crew was making ready to sail back to Europe. After the shipwreck, Joanes de Portu of San Sebastián, the owner of the *Nuestra Señora de la Conçeçion*, salvaged the sails, some rope and victuals, rescued most of the crew, and then returned home. The cargo was partly insured, and it is from the harpooners' insurance claims that the events of the shipwreck have been reconstructed. Canadian Parks Service marine archaeologists recently con-

41 Iñaki Zumalde, "Tras las hellas de los balleneros vascos en Terranova," *Deia* (March 23, 1980), p. 4.

42 Mariano Ciriquiain Gaiztarro, "Los Vascos en...," *op. cit.*, p. 184.

43 The first known will in Canadian history was written by Domingo de Miranda, in Trepassey [Trespas] in 1549. The Basque Country. AGDG. Tolosa. Corregimiento, Civiles Mandiola, Legajo 339.

44 Martin de Hoyarsabal, *Les voyages aventureux du capitaine Martin Hoyarsabal, habitant de Çubiburu* (Bordeaux: Guillaume Millanges, 1633), p. 109-114. The variants Butus, Buetes, Buytres and Butes are also found in the documents.

45 René Bélanger, *op. cit.*, p. 46.

ducted work at the wreck site,[46] and the discovery of the *San Juan* has led to the development of a wide-ranging program of multidisciplinary research which has made it possible to reconstruct in some detail a whaling expedition to Labrador in the second half of the 16th century.

46 Selma Barkham and Robert Grenier, "Divers Find Sunken Basque Galleon in Labrador," *Canadian Geographical Journal*, Vol. 97, No. 3 (Dec. 78-Jan. 79), p. 61. Since 1978, the year marking the beginning of the underwater archaeological excavations in Red Bay, three more sunken galleons have been discovered by divers, along with the remains of four small boats. See: Robert Grenier and James A. Tuck, "Discovery in Labrador: a 16th-Century Basque Whaling Port and its Sunken Fleet," *National Geographic* (July 1985), pp. 40-71.

Chapter II
Methods and Technology of the Whale Hunt

The history of the Basque lands, like that of certain northern European countries, was determined over the course of several centuries by the sea. Unable to rely on their hinterland with its fragile and undiversified economy, very early on in their history the Basques turned for their subsistence to the sea, and they became the first people to transform the whale fishery into an industry operating on an international scale.

One somewhat fanciful view is that the Basques discovered the great value of whales while using arrows and spears to chase off the ones that kept destroying their fishing nets![1] Finding the whales to be timid and harmless creatures, they were emboldened to attack them with harpoons, and thus was born, in this view, the renowned Basque whaling industry.

A more plausible explanation is that the Basques learned their whaling technique from the Vikings. As a result of internal troubles in their own lands in the 8th century, the Vikings invaded northern France, where they called themselves Normans. This southward migration soon turned into a movement of conquest that reached as far as Gascony, which the Vikings occupied until the 10th century. They practised whaling along the coasts of Normandy and Aquitaine, and the Basques, in this view,

1 William Scoresby, *The Arctic Regions and the Northern Whale-Fishery* (London: The Religious Tract Society, [183?], p. 11. Note that this is not Scoresby's own view, which indeed he contradicts.

learned the art when they came in contact with them.[2] However it would be an exaggeration to say that the Basques simply copied Scandinavian methods. In their homeland, the Vikings caught whales by guiding them into the numerous deep fjords along the coast, and in Normandy they drove them onto shoals where the whales became beached and were then killed. Since similar geographical features did not exist along the Basque coast, the Basques had to learn to catch whales on the high seas. This involved so many changes in methods of capture and in technology that we are justified in speaking of indigenous Basque techniques. This is probably what has led many writers to believe that the Basques did not borrow their whaling methods and technology from other peoples, and were in fact the real innovators in this field.[3] The truth is that the Basques never kept to a single approach; they were always able to adapt their whaling technique to varying conditions such as accessibility to ports, distance from the coast, type of ocean bottom, winds and currents, etc. It is in this sense that the Basques are the true initiators of the methods that would be used over the course of many centuries by all of the whaling nations.

From the 11th to the 15th centuries, the Basques hunted whale in the Gulf of Biscay. Then, for the reasons discussed in Chapter I, they began to pursue their quarry out onto the high seas. This eventually led them to America, where they employed essentially the same techniques they had been using at home for centuries. Only the equipment had to be modified, to adapt it to the new conditions in Labrador.

The Whaling Ships

One of the changes necessitated by expeditions to America concerned the whaling ships themselves.[4] With the advent of long-haul journeys lasting several months, larger vessels were needed in order to cope with the sea and carry more equipment and larger crews. The Basques had no problem adapting to these new conditions since they were in the vanguard of shipbuilding technology. Using local resources that provided most of the materials they needed, the southern

2 E.J. Slijper, *Whales* (London: Hutchinson, 1962), p. 17.

3 Marcel A. Hérubel, *op. cit.*, p. 605 and Mariano Ciriquiain Gaiztarro, "Los Vascos en...," *op. cit.*, p. 72.

4 Details of the architecture of Basque whalers will be analysed in a later study.

Basques were building some of the vessels being used for the great armadas and for the Indies trade just as the northern Basques were filling orders for the king of France. Historian Jacques Bernard has discovered documents in the Bordeaux notarial archives which show that this city too was turning to the Basques for complex shipbuilding work.[5]

Yet despite their expertise, the Basques did not create a new kind of ship for whaling purposes. Rather they adapted the ships they already possessed depending on need and circumstance. There were many types of ship, designated by a great variety of names based on function or structure or rigging or other features. For whaling purposes, the point was to arrive at the right compromise between capacity, cruising speed and safety.

For expeditions to Terranova, the Basques seem to prefer galleons, if we can judge by archival charter contracts.[6] This type of ship seems to have appeared as a result of repeated attacks by privateers against ships engaged in the Indies trade. Jacques Bernard calls them "descendants of the medieval galley," and they were a cross between a galley and a 15th-century whaling ship.[7] Being of greater tonnage than other ships, they did not have to make as many trips, thus reducing the risk of capture. The galleons of the southern Basques often had a capacity of 200 *toneladas* or more.[8] Some like the *Santa Ana* of Joanes de Portu were as much as 650 *toneladas*.

---

5 Jacques Bernard, "Les constructions navales à Bordeaux d'après les archives notariales du XVIe siècle," in *Travaux du Colloque international d'histoire maritime* (1st, Paris, 1956) [Paris: S.E.V.P.E.N., 1957], p. 32.

6 Michael Barkham, "Report on 16th Century Spanish Basque Shipbuilding, ca. 1550 to ca. 1600," Manuscript Report Series No. 422 (Ottawa: Parks Canada, 1981), p. 4. The meaning of the term galleon becomes more precise in the second half of the 16th century. Whereas at first it was used to designate small vessels of barely 10 or 20 tons, around 1570 it came to be used only for large carriers.

7 Jacques Bernard, "Les types de navire ibériques et leur influence sur la construction navale dans les ports du sud-ouest de la France, XVe-XVIe siècles," in *Travaux du Colloque international d'histoire maritime* (5th, Lisbon, 1960) [Paris: S.E.V.P.E.N., 1960], p. 205. Bernard specifies that the French words "galion" [galleon] and "galère" [galley] are sometimes used synonymously in the Bordeaux archives documents of the 16th century. The same is true of documents in the Basque archives — lawyers use the words *nao*, *navio* and *galeon* without distinction to designate a single ship, often in the same document.

8 The *tonelada* was a measurement of tonnage based on the principal dimensions of the ship. It was equivalent to 1.51 cubic metres, and was thus quite similar to the old Bordeaux *tonneau*, which was 1.44 cubic metres. The method of calculating tonnage set out by Cristobal de Barros in 1590 consisted in multiplying half the beam of the ship by its length and its depth, reducing the result by five percent and dividing by eight Multiplying the three dimensions, expressed in cubits of 57.46 cm, yielded the internal volume of the ship, with each *tonelada* being eight cubic cubits (hence the division by eight in the method of calculation). This formula is confirmed in the documents from a trial held in 1585 concerning the tonnage of two ships. The Basque Country. AGDG. Tolosa. Corregimiento, Ejecutivos Mandiola, Legajo 162.

If the ships could carry about three barrels of whale oil per *tonelada*, the biggest of them would be able to transport in their holds some 2000 barrels, each containing 211 litres and weighing about 182 kilograms. The ships of the northern Basques generally had lower tonnages because of the shallow water in their ports.

The notarial archives of the southern Basque country contain a wealth of valuable information on the architecture of these ships, usually contained in construction contracts that were signed by the parties and witnesses and notarized. The documents first identify the two parties — the owner or owners and the master shipwright. They then specify the ship's dimensions, the type and quality of materials to be used, the arrangement of the various parts of the ship, and the deadlines for carrying out the work and for delivery of equipment and materials. Sometimes the cubit measure used in a particular locality is specified, and even the origin of the materials. The documents generally end with a clause on the method of payment. This usually involved three payments: the first when the master carpenter laid the keel; the second when he had finished putting down the planking; and the third on launch day. Finally, the contracts provide penalties to be levied against parties failing to meet their obligations.

Generally speaking, with ships of over 200 *toneladas* the length of the keel proper was equal to or slightly less than double that of the midship beam. As for the length overall, it was 1.6 times that of the keel. According to the first Spanish ship construction treatise, written in 1587 by Diego Garcia de Palacio, a scholar and advisor to the king, a *nao* of 400 *toneladas* should have a keel of 34 cubits from stem to stern, be 16 cubits wide and 11½ cubits deep. The hold should be 4 to 4½ cubits high — the height of three *pipas* [large casks] — and the first deck three cubits high. The mainmast should have square sails — main course, topsail and topgallant — and be equal in length to the keel together with the rake, which was generally longer in Basque ships than in other European vessels. The foremast, to be rigged like the mainmast, should be equal in length to the keel proper. The bowsprit, with its spritsail yard and hanging sail, should be 0.8 of the length of the foremast and equal in length to the mizzen mast with its lateen sail. These dimensions could vary, however, depending on the builder and the available wood. Galleons were made almost entirely of oak and had four anchors of 16 to 18 quintals [hundredweight] each.[9] One

9 Cesareo Fernandez Duro, *Disquisiciones náuticas* (Madrid: Impresor de Camara de SM, 1881), Vol. 6, p. 8.

historian has estimated that the maximum lifetime of these ships in the 16th century was 13 years.[10] Once they had made two or three trips to Terranova or to Northern Europe, they were generally sold to Seville before ending their days in the West Indies. In winter and spring, the ships may also have been used for whaling off the Galician coast or for the home trade along the coast while awaiting the next season.[11]

Financing the Expedition

In his *Recueil des voyages au Nord*, published in 1715, Bernard states that those undertaking to outfit one or several vessels for whaling have to begin work in the autumn in order to be ready by the next spring.[12] The *Recueil* deals with Dutch whaling at Spitsbergen and in the Arctic during the 18th century. However since whaling methods remained almost unchanged until the mid 19th century, the preparatory stage must have been basically identical two centuries earlier when the Basques were going to America.

The first step was to find the capital necessary to outfit the ship. The owner or outfitter had to borrow money, and the loan often had to be underwritten by an insurer. Because of the high cost involved, typically equal to the value of the ship itself, several investors generally joined together to amass the necessary funds. For example in 1565 Pedro de Guarnizo, Sebastian de Correbedo and Sebastian de Uryeta shared the 3170 ducat cost of outfitting the *Santo Crucifixo de Burgos*.[13] This practice of joint investment was dictated by prudence: it was better that an investor's portfolio contain shares in several expeditions rather than having everything invested in a single expedition. If the whaling was bad, or the ship sustained damages or sank, the loss could be recovered from other more fruitful ventures. In France, it was the custom to use a bottomry bond. In this type of arrangement, the lenders advanced the amounts needed for outfitting, *en espèces sonnantes et trébuchantes* [in coin of the realm]. The loan period was the duration of the expedition, so repayment was expected only when the ship returned, at which time the borrowers would hand over the

10 Laurier Turgeon, "Pêches basques...," *op. cit.*, p. 296, note 38.
11 Jacques Bernard, *Navires...*, *op. cit.*, p. 822.
12 Michel Vaucaire, *Histoire de la pêche de la baleine* (Paris: Payot, 1941), p. 132.
13 The Basque Country. AGDG. Tolosa. Corregimiento, Civiles Elorza, Legajo 213, fol. 25r.

capital advanced plus interest of as much as 15 to 30 percent. If the ship was lost, the borrowers did not have to repay the loan, which explains why in French these were called loans *à la grosse aventure* [high risk].[14] This method of financing was also used in Spain.

As in France, lenders assumed all the risk from the day of the ship's departure until 24 hours after it returned to its home port. In exchange, borrowers agreed to hand over a certain number of barrels of oil corresponding to the amount advanced, plus a percentage of the profits.[15] If the hold was full, the outfitters would simply give the lender the agreed number of barrels of oil plus a percentage of the income However the situation would be considerably more complicated if, as often happened, the whaler returned with less than a full hold. Custom then stipulated that the borrower must reimburse the lender in proportion to the cargo: if a ship with a capacity of 1000 barrels brought back only 500, the outfitters would hand over half the agreed number of barrels and they did not have to reimburse the difference either in money or in kind. In practice, such cases gave rise to much litigation among outfitters, owners and lenders, with each party trying to find the loophole in the law that would give them the maximum profit on their investment.[16] Of course if the ship had sunk, as with Andres de Alcola's vessel which went down at Fuenterrabia in 1596 the lender lost all his capital, since he had assumed the risk *sobre la quilla* [on the keel].[17] The risk was thus similar to that involved in the French *grosse aventure* contract.[18]

14 Laurier Turgeon, "Les pêches françaises à terreneuve d'après les archives notariales de Bordeaux: 1555-1614," paper read at the 11th Congress of the French Historical Society, Québec, May 9-11, 1985, p. 22.

15 In 1572, the *San Nicolas* belonging to Nicolas de Segura made a profit of 15 percent. Thirty years earlier, in 1542, a ship belonging to Francisco de Aganduru made 30 percent. The literature does not reveal whether these were normal profits for their respective periods. Spain. Valladolid. Archivo de la Real Chancilleria (henceforth ARC). Pleitos civiles. Perez Alonzo fenecidos, Legajo 977-3. The Basque Country. AGDG. Tolosa, Corregimiento, Civiles Mandiola, Legajo 77, fol. 23v.

16 A very large number of such trials are documented in the archives of Tolosa and Valladolid — an invaluable mine of information.

17 The Spanish expression is probably based on the fact that the ship was deemed to be a total loss if the keel could not be recovered. The Basque Country. AGDG. Tolosa. Corregimiento, Civiles Elorza, Legajo 216.

18 According to the archival documents, it appears that in certain specific cases the lender could require full reimbursement of the number of barrels specified in the contract regardless of what cargo was brought back. Spain. Valladolid. ARC. Pleitos civiles, Masas fenecidos, Legajo 511-3.

Preparing the Ship

Once the funds had been found, the owner and the outfitter would sign a rental agreement defining the responsibilities of each party. Several such contracts can be found in notarial archives in both the northern and southern Basque country, and they constitute a rich source of information on how whaling was organized at this time. The contracts generally have three parts. First, the parties are identified. Then the obligation of the owner to provide a properly rigged ship in good condition is set out. The owner also had to select some of the key crew members, such as the master, boatswain, pilot, harpooners and steward, and pay a portion of their bonuses. In addition, the owner had to provide the artillery, arms and ammunition necessary for the journey. In the second part of the contract, the outfitter agrees to provide the rest of the crew, pay their wages and furnish victuals and equipment for a season of about nine months. Finally, the contract sets out how the take will be shared. The owner generally got a quarter of the oil and of the booty from captured ships, the crew a third and the outfitter the remainder.

Under these agreements, the prime task of the owner was to prepare the ship for the expedition. In a contract signed at Bilbao on January 17, 1564, between Gonzalo de Landaverde, owner of the galleon *San Nicolas*, and Juan de Espilla, his captain, the owner undertook to have the work done "from keel to mast-head ... and in the manner required for such a voyage."[19] The work consisted in repairing the keel, caulking the sides and decks, and supplying cabling, stays, sails, tackle, masts, anchors and all necessary cordage. The terms of the contract even provided for pitch and oakum, so that the ship could be overhauled before leaving Terranova for the return journey.

Arming the Ship

The owner was also responsible for arming the ship. Purchase and maintenance of weapons increased the outfitting cost but were essential for defence not only against enemy privateers — which according to records of the deliberations of the town of

19 René Bélanger, *op. cit.*, p. 105.

Bayonne were roving the waters off Terranova as early as 1528 — but also against Basques from the opposite side of the French-Spanish border.[20] When France and Spain declared war in 1542, the Basques often took the opportunity to attack each other. For example a French expedition in 1554 captured four Spanish whalers in Labrador.[21] In response, Philip II of Spain issued an ordinance, on April 21, 1557, that all ships leaving for Terranova must be armed. Although it was revoked a few months later, the practice of arming ships was maintained, as shown by copious documentary evidence of arms being loaded on board whalers. The arms may also have served for self-defence against the native peoples along the Labrador coast, with whom relations were not always amicable.

The minimum weaponry that had to be placed on board the ships included four iron cannons and eight swivel guns.[22] In 1550, the 130-*tonelada* ship *Madalena* was carrying six *bombardas* [cannons] and eight *versos* [swivel guns], while the 650-*tonelada Santa Ana* had 10 cannons and 20 swivel guns.[23] The galleon *San Nicolas* had six large pieces and 12 swivel guns, as did the *Nuestra Señora de Yciar.*[24] In addition to this heavy weaponry, there were also arquebuses, crossbows, picks, spears and the crew members' personal firearms. Thus armed, the whalers could respond to any attack, and where necessary serve as privateers, as in the case of the *Sancti Spiritus* in 1554.[25]

The Whaling Gear

While the owner was responsible for preparing and arming the ship itself, the outfitter had to provide the whaling gear and supplies. The outfitter would often delegate his powers to the captain of the vessel (when he was not himself the captain). In 1564, Captain Juan de Espilla agreed to provide the *San Nicolas* with cauldrons, lines, ladles, harpoons, lances, barrels, catcher boats and other

20 Édouard Ducéré, "Recherches historiques...," *op. cit.*, p. 219.

21 Selma Barkham, "Documentary evidence...," *op. cit.*, p. 58.

22 *Ibid.*, p. 57.

23 *Ibid.*, p. 56.

24 René Bélanger, *op. cit.*, p. 105.

25 The Basque Country. Archivo Historico de los Protocolos de Guipuzcoa (henceforth AHPG), Oñate, Partido de Vergara, vol. 2596, fol. 51r-56v.

necessities.[26] A very similar division of responsibilities is found in a charter party between Bartolome de Garro and Juanes de Eleyçamendi concerning the provisioning of the *Trinidad* for a whaling expedition to Terranova in 1574.[27] When there was more than one outfitter, as in the case of the *Catalina de San Juan* in 1596, each was assigned a share of the responsiblities in proportion to their investment.[28]

Whether in America or along the shores of the Gulf of Biscay, the key item of equipment was the catcher boat, also called a whaleboat or shallop. The historical documents are almost silent on this subject, and descriptions of the boats vary considerably from one writer to another. For example, in the early 17th century Martinez de Isasti wrote that they could carry 12 to 15 men, whereas the 20th-century historian Ciriquiain Gaiztarro mentions three men.[29] All the documents on the subject date from the 17th, 18th and 19th centuries. Even illustrations do not help because they are imprecise, based on Dutch experience, and reveal no typical size (they show boats manned by 8, 6, 5, 4 or even 2 men). Dégros claims that the catcher boats were identical to the boats used along the Basque coast, but bigger and sturdier. He describes them as being built with oak frames and fir planking, with inclined stem and stern posts, and as being 8 metres long, 2 m wide and 1 m deep.[30] Bélanger mentions a French document in the Bayonne municipal archives which contains probably the most detailed description we have:

> *To pursue and overtake the whale, vessels are employed which are of very small scantling and thus very light, called Boat in English and Pirogue in French. Usually they are 7 metres in length and 1 metre 70 or 80c. in breadth, with a depth of 40 to 45c. at the centre and over one metre at the ends, which gives them a strongly arched appearance. The frames are barely more than 1c. and a half thick, and the planking, which is of cedar, at most 1c thick. Sharp and tapered at the ends, but flat toward the centre, the boat is propelled by 5 oars and by a Stern Oar, a steering oar which serves*

26 René Bélanger, *op. cit.*, p. 105.

27 Selma Barkham, "Documentary evidence...," *op. cit.*, p. 81.

28 The Basque Country. AGDG. Tolosa. Corregimiento, Civiles Lecuona, Legajo 9, file 219.

29 Mariano Ciriquiain Gaiztarro, *op. cit.*, p. 88.

30 Maxime Dégros, *op. cit.*, No. 43 (1943), p. 58. A French document from 1565 mentions a *chaluppe* [shallop] of 15.5 *aunes* [ells], that is, 18.3 metres. France. Bordeaux. Archives départementales de la Gironde (henceforth ADG). Notaire Brigot, 3E2418, fol. 181.

as a rudder and is therefore positioned at the stern parallel to the length of the craft. Also at the stern is a short decking or cuddy board in which is housed a fixed wooden post shaped like a capstan and called a Loggerhead. The oars are placed in wooden oarlocks with a thrum mat covering to prevent noise. Three of the oars are about 4m. 65 in length, the fourth is 5m. 30c and the fifth 4m. 30c; the Stern Oar is about 6m long. The oars are made of ash and are of excellent quality. Once the oars are shipped, their handles can be inserted in a hole in the cleat nailed to the stringers at the rower's feet, so that the oars will sit apeak when at rest. At the bow there is another cuddy board, but smaller than the one at the stern, and with a half-moon notch in it. A square groove lined with lead is cut through the stem. The boats all have a hole in one of the bottom planks, either foreward or aft, to let water drain out.[31]

Now this is a description of the catcher boats used for deep-sea whaling in the early 19th century. There is, therefore, theoretically a certain risk in applying the description to 16th-century boats, but in fact the risk is rather small in view of the slow development of whaling technology over time as well as the recent findings at the excavation site at Red Bay, Labrador, where archaeologists have found what appear to be the remains of two shallops under the wreck of the *San Juan*. An initial cursory

31 René Bélanger, *op. cit.*, p. 121. In size and shape this kind of vessel resembles those used by the Americans in the 19th century. They were 8.4 m to 9 m in length with a beam of 1.8 m and a depth of 55 cm at the middle and 92.5 cm at the extremities. "It is sharp at both ends, with flaring sides, and is of a model that insures great swiftness, as well as the qualities of an excellent seaboat. At the bow is a groove, in which is placed a metal sheave, over which the line runs; near the end and upper edges of the groove, a slender pin, of tough wood or whalebone, passes across through holes above the line, to prevent it from flying out when running. This groove is called the 'chocks'. About three feet from the stern is the clumsy-cleet, a stout thwart with a rounded notch on the after side, in which the officer or boat-steerer braces himself by one leg against the violent motion of the boat, caused by a rough sea, or the efforts of the whale while being worked upon. The space between the clumsy-cleet and the chocks is covered with a sort of deck, six inches below the gunwales, and is called the box, or box of the boat. Five thwarts, or seats, for the accommodation of the rowers, are placed at proper distances apart, between the clumsy-cleet and stern sheets; and opposite each rowlock, near the bottom of the boat, is a well-fastened cleet, to receive the end or handle of the oar, which is called a peak-cleet; and when fast to a whale, or when the crew are resting, the end of the oar is placed in the hole of this cleet, while the heavy portion still rests in the rowlock, thereby elevating the blade far above the water. About four feet of the stern is decked over, through the forward part of which, a little to one side, is placed the loggerhead, shaped like a post with a large head, which projects six or eight inches above the gunwhales, and by this loggerhead the line is controlled when the boat is fast to the object of pursuit." Charles M. Scammon, *The Marine Mammals of the Northwestern Coast of North America Described and Illustrated; Together with an Account of the American Whale-fishery* (New York: Dover Publication, 1968), p. 224.

examination reveals that they correspond very closely to the above description. They were 8.2 metres long, they were equipped with sails, and they had six thwarts for the rowers. The arched keel would increase manoeuvrability while the tapered form, identical at both ends, would facilitate rapid changes in direction. Reinforcement of the planking would provide resistance to waves during the chase. The upper two strakes were clinker-built and the others carvel-built. While of sturdy construction, these boats do not have the reinforcement that would have been needed to lower them into the water from the ship, as was later the practice in deep-sea whaling. They have many points in common with the boats used at Santander and Bermeo during the period of inshore whaling along the Basque coast.[32]

In the 16th century, each ship would have had up to 10 craft of this type, depending on its size. They were called by various names: shallops, pinnaces, boats, *biscayennes, pirogues* or whaleboats.[33] During the crossing, they remained disassembled and stacked one inside the other because of the restricted space available. They were stowed under the upper deck on the starboard side and were not put into the water until the ship reached its destination.

The whaleboats would certainly have had to be equipped with a fairly full assortment of whaling gear. Bélanger mentions a copper compass, an *escap* [scoop] to bail water, a small chest [?], a boat hook, a flagstaff, a spritsail, a grapnel and a water-

32 An ordinance issued by the brotherhood of whalers of Bermeo in 1353, which sets at 18 short cubits [*petite coudée = 0.450 m*] the minimum length of boats permitted to have sails, states that shallops — described as being designed for speed and manoeuvrability — had to be at least 7.7 metres long, 1.8 metres wide and 1 metre deep. The keel is described as not prominent and as being arched — higher in the middle than at the ends. Both stem and stern curve to a point. The boat is made of oak, carvel-built, barely 1 cm thick. The paired oars are 4 metres in length and pass through a rope or leather strop attached to the oarlock, which is slotted into the gunwale and fitted with a lining of rope and grease to silence the noise. A stern oar 5 or 6 metres in length enables precise manoeuvring. There are sails so that the rowers can rest during long trips. A central mast supports a square sail or spritsail, while a foresail facilitates manoeuvring. Mariano Ciriquiain Gaiztarro, "Las primeras representaciones gráficas de embarcaciones del litoral vasco," *Boletin de la Real Sociedada Vascongada de los amigos del país,* Vol. 10 (1954), p. 68. This description also fits the shallops of Santander very closely. They had keels of 14 to 16 cubits (6.5 metres), with a beam of 7 feet (2.1 metres) and a depth of 3 feet (90 cm). They had 7 or 8 thwarts and used a main sail and a foresail, probably both square. José L. Casado Soto, *Los pescadores de la villa de Santander...* (Santander: no publisher, 1978), p. 47.

33 The *nao* belonging to Francisco de Elorriaga carried four whaleboats in 1565. The Basque Country. AGDG. Tolosa. Corregimiento, Civiles Elorza, Legajo 65, fol. 20r. However the next year, Captain Miguel de Cerain asked for 10 boats which he apparently placed aboard the *Nuestra Señora de la Guadelupe.* Spain. Valladolid. ARC. Pleitos civiles, Masas fenecidos 260-61, box 1045-1. According to René Bélanger, these are the boats that would later be known in Eastern Canada as dories. René Bélanger, *op. cit.,* p. 2.

tight cask or [?] containing a lantern, candles, stones, flint, kindling and matches. Provisions would include biscuit, and sometimes cheese and fresh water.[34] Note however that the text Bélanger cites describes boats used for deep-sea whaling, where the risk of getting lost at sea was much greater (hence the compass, the beacon and the provisions). In the case of the Basques in Labrador, the risk was much smaller since the whalemen stayed in sight of shore. To the extent that a risk existed, the safety equipment would certainly have been less comprehensive.

The Basques also brought to Labrador another type of craft, whose existence has been revealed for the first time during the archaeological excavations at Red Bay. It had oars and sails, and a keel of about 11 metres according to initial measurements taken by the divers at the wreck site. This is three or four metres longer than a shallop keel. But what was it used for? If it was used to chase and capture whales, then the discovery at Red Bay of a pinnace, if that is what it is, calls into question all our assumptions about 16th-century Basque whaling methods. If all the shallops of the period were this size, then a galleon like the *San Juan*, with its keel of just under 15 metres, could not possibly have carried a half-dozen of them, as described in later documents. Thus we are left with two problems: how were these vessels transported to Labrador, and what were they used for if not for whale-hunting?

It is, of course, possible that the pinnace was disassembled and then loaded on the ship, but this is unlikely. Given their relative sizes, it is hard to see how a galleon like the *San Juan* could have held such a craft. Since the ship had to carry the shallops as well as equipment and enough provisions for a crew of 75 men for nine months, available free space must have been extremely limited. It is equally unlikely that the pinnace crossed the ocean on its own: how could a deckless 11-metre vessel deal with the storms of the North Atlantic and the Strait of Belle Isle? The logical conclusion is that the pinnaces were towed by the galleons, a method the Basques had already been using during the period of inshore whaling along the Galician coast. Divers working at the wreck of the *San Juan* discovered a piece of wood from the ship which was engraved. It showed a galleon at anchor with another vessel attached by a line.

As to the role of these pinnaces, one view is that they were used, as in Europe, to provide links among the various ports in Labrador, to bring in fresh food and equipment,

34 René Bélanger, *op. cit.*, p. 121.

and perhaps even to trade with the natives while the galleon stood at anchor in a harbour. This had already been the practice among cod-fishermen, and was later used by the colonizers La Roche, Du Gua de Monts and Champlain.

The Basques were very conservative in their use of whaling gear. Descriptions of the gear (as used by the Basques and then by others) remain almost unchanged from the 16th to the 19th century. Whalemen had no incentive to improve their equipment because whales were so abundant, at least in the better years. The harpoon remained the basic tool. The kind used in Labrador was essentially the same as that employed several centuries earlier along the Basque coast, as is confirmed by archaeological discoveries in ports along the Strait of Belle Isle. The barb had the shape of an inverted V that became thicker as it approached the point where it joined the 1 cm-round, malleable iron, stem. This part of the harpoon, called the head, was 65 cm long and terminated in a 30 cm socket into which was inserted the shank. The beech shank measured 1.65 metres in length by 4 cm in diameter. It was secured by a line attached to the socket and extending two-thirds of the way down the length of the shank, where it was held by a number of yarn fastenings."[35] This line, called a fore-goer, was about 13 metres long and was left untarred so that it would not be stiff. It ended in a loop to which the main whale line was attached. This setup made it possible to recover the shank after the head of the harpoon had lodged in the whale's body and become detached.[36]

To kill the whale a lance was used. It was constructed on the same principle as the harpoon, but its shape and size were different. The ovular tip was like a spatula, and the head was longer than a harpoon's — 1.5 to 1.6 metres. It terminated in a socket into which was inserted a wooden shank about 2.5 metres long and 3 cm in diameter. As with the harpoon, the shank was secured by a line, but in this case the line extended the full length of the shank. It was 15 metres long and was used

35 *Ibid.* p. 122. These dimensions are slightly larger than those mentioned in Sañez Reguart's dictionary, cited by Ciriquiain Gaiztarro. The latter mentions, however, that the harpoons used in Terranova must have been a little bigger than those described by Sañez Reguart, because in a Lequeitio document of 1555 there is mention of a "jabalin grande de nueva suerte, de Terra Nueva" (new type of long spear, of Terranova). Mariano Ciriquiain Gaiztarro, *Los Vascos..., op. cit.*, p. 90.

36 Sañez Reguart mentions a second harpoon, identical to the first but used to slow the animal down. It was attached, by a line 8 metres to 10 metres in length, to a wooden buoy imprinted with the name of the ship. It was apparently used in Spitsbergen. Antonio Sañez Reguart, *Diccionario historico de las artes de la pesca nacional por el Comisario Real de Guerra y de marina* (Madrid: no publisher, 1795), p. 372.

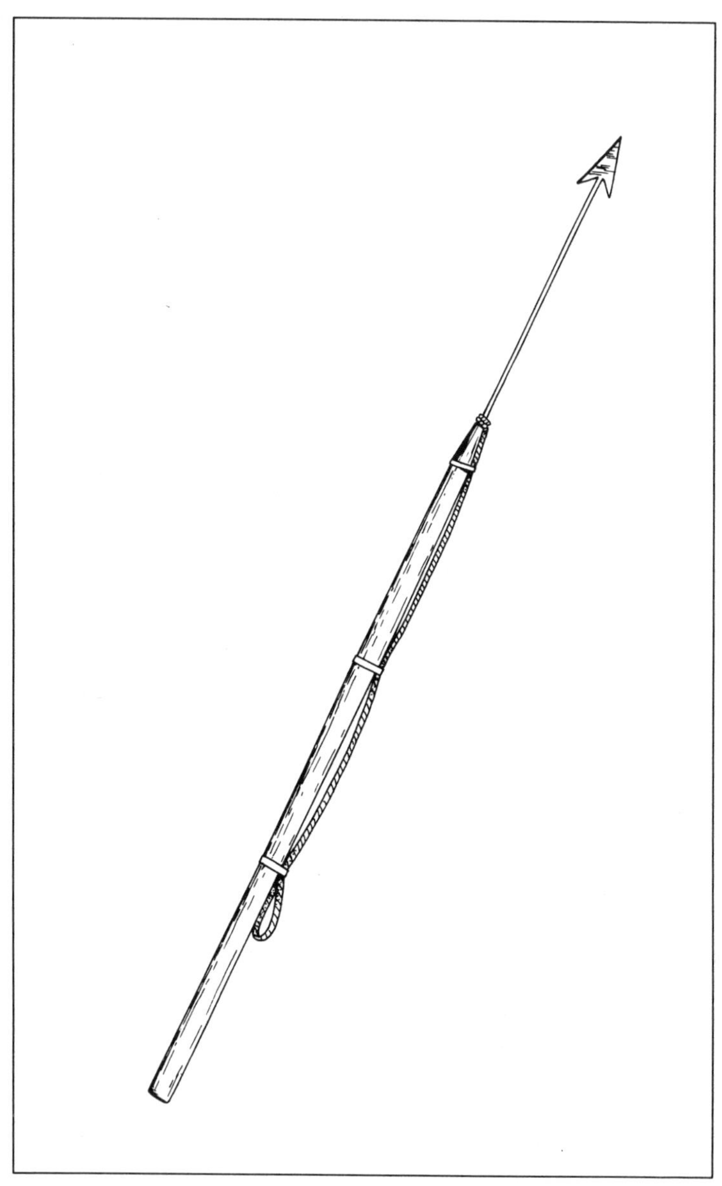

5. A Basque harpoon. *Drawing: Dorothea Kappler.*

to retrieve the lance from the whale's body. As with the harpoon, the end of the lance was waxed so that the men would not be wounded if they touched it, and to protect it from the sea water.

With regards to the main lines, each boat carried two, 16 mm in diameter and 150 metres long. If necessary the men could easily splice them together. They were kept coiled in a wooden basin or tub at the back of the boat, and they were connected to the harpoon line by a loop.[37] A 19th-century document describes the placing of the line as follows:

> *The bottom end of the line comes back up to the top of the tub and terminates in a loop. The top end goes once around the small fixed capstan already described, and is then passed over the oars and inserted in the lead-lined groove in the stem, care being taken to place a wooden pin above the line to prevent it from flying out. This end of the line then goes to the cuddy board, where it forms a coil 4 or 5 fathoms long, before continuing to the place where it is attached, by a sheet bend, to one of the harpoons that is kept armed at the very front of the boat and is positioned so that the head lies on a small cleat and the shank on a crutch. Another line, five or six fathoms in length, is attached at one end to the second harpoon, also by a sheet bend, while the other end of this line forms a slip knot and is thereby attached to the line that goes to the first harpoon....*[38]

In addition to the gear directly related to catching the whales, outfitters had to provide the equipment needed to try the blubber and store the oil. At the top of the list came the materials for building shelters and trying ovens. For this purpose the Basques took along nails, clay and tiles. According to insurance claims made by captain Miguel de Cerain, in 1566 the *Nuestra Señora de Guadelupe* of Bilbao carried 20 barrels of earth and 6000 tiles to construct ovens in Labrador.[39] As the presence of nails attests, the uprights of these structures were made of wood found by the men locally. Regarding the cauldrons, the number most often mentioned in the documents

37 Spain. Valladolid. ARC, Pleitos civiles, Masus fenecidas, box 1045-1. According to the ordinance issued at Lequeitio in 1555, the line had to be 70 fathoms long (177 metres) and be composed of 30 strands. The document does not specify whether the lines in question are those used in Terranova or along the Basque coast. Mariano Ciriquiain Gaiztarro, *Los Vascos...*, *op. cit.*, p. 93.

38 René Bélanger, *op. cit.*, p. 123.

39 Spain. Valladolid. ARC. Pleitos civiles. Masas fenecidos, box 1045-1.

is four.[40] The outfitter also had to provide pre-constructed barrels to store the oil. The number would vary with the tonnage of the ship. A 300-ton ship would normally carry about a thousand 211-litre barrels. On the outbound trip, some of these may have been assembled to contain victuals and ballast, while the rest were carried in pieces. This is what is suggested by a 1725 document which speaks of 4000 barrels "both empty and filled" and 2000 others "in bundles."[41] One of the functions of the cooper upon arrival was to assemble the components of the barrels by following marks which the manufacturers had placed on the oak covers and staves.

Aside from all this, a host of other objects associated directly or indirectly with the whaling work had to be taken along, from simple table knives to a large saw, wax candles for light, bowls, pestles, earthenware jars and so forth.[42]

The Victuals

It was also up to the outfitter to ship provisions, which would have to have been quite considerable in quantity to feed a crew for eight or nine months. So far, however, research has turned up few complete, detailed lists of the provisions loaded on Basque whalers bound for Labrador. We have only indirect information from trials, charter parties and hiring contracts. Generally speaking, these documents reveal that the selection of food was limited and quantities would have been insufficient had they not been extended by local supplies of salmon, cod, birds and even polar bears obtained in Terranova. When the ships left Europe for an eight-month trip, they would normally carry wheat to make biscuit, bacon, beans, peas, olive oil, mustard seed, sardines, sherry, cider, flour and garlic. Obviously the quantities would vary depending on the number of crew members. In the case of the 1566 voyage of the *Nuestra Señora de Guadelupe*, with 100 men aboard, the ship was carrying 750 bushels *[hanegas]* of wheat to make biscuit, 8 quintals of bacon, 14 bushels of broad beans, 14 bushels of peas, 8 quintals of olive oil, 2 bushels of mustard seed, 6 quintals of cod, 4000 sardines, 8 butts (casks) of sherry, 120 butts

40 Selma Barkham, "Documentary evidence...", *op. cit.,* p. 77.

41 Éric Dardel, *op. cit.,* p. 130.

42 Mariano Ciriquiain Gaiztarro, *Los Vascos..., op. cit.,* p. 277. The Basque Country. AHPG. Oñate. Partido de Vergara, Vol. 2580, reg. 4, fol. 9v. Michael Barkham, *Aspects of life..., op. cit.,* p. 19.

[botas] of cider, 4 bushels of flour and some garlic.[43] In that same year, the whaler *Nuestra Señora de la Conçeçion*, which was slightly smaller, carried 560 bushels of wheat, 5½ shoulders or haunches of bacon, 15 bushels of broad beans, 30 *arrobas* of olive oil, ½ bushel of mustard seed, 40 butts of Puerto Real wine, 200 hogsheads *[barricas]* of Fuenterrabia cider and 5 bushels of flour.[44]

The following quantities of foodstuffs appear to have been carried on southern Basque whalers. These figures are necessarily based on guesswork because of the very limited data available:

Biscuit	675 g (per man per day)
Bacon	14 g
Beans	28 g
Peas	28 g
Wine	300 mL
Cider	2500 mL

If this is correct, it would seem that quantities of some items were far from sufficient. This is notably the case with the bacon. According to one historian, it would have been necessary to add a further 200 to 450 grams of meat to bring the ration up to 16th-century levels.[45] Presumably the extra animal protein was obtained through hunting and fishing, as suggested by the excavations at Red Bay where archaeologists have discovered many remains of local fauna. And it would certainly be surprising if the whalemen did not make use of the thousands of kilograms of meat available from a single captured whale.

The northern Basques had essentially the same diet except that the cider was replaced by wine. Jacques Bernard mentions some examples for the period 1539-50. In 1539, the *Seraine* of Bourg had a crew of 28 and the outfitter was required to supply 1 pipe (large cask) of wine, 3 quintals of biscuit and a half side of bacon *[demy lart]*

43 Spain. Valladolid. ARC. Pleitos civiles, Masas fenecidos, box 1045-1. The *hanega* varied from region to region but was generally 55.5 litres. The 16th-century quintal was 100 pounds except that a quintal of iron was 150 pounds.

44 *Idem.* An *arroba* of oil was 12.56 litres, while an *arroba* of wine was 16.14 litres. The ship's biscuit had a very high protein, phosphorus and vitamin B content. Generally speaking, one *hanega* of wheat would make 50 pounds of biscuit.

45 L. Denoix, "Caractéristiques des navires de l'époque des grandes découvertes," in *Travaux du Colloque international d'histoire maritime* (5th, Lisbon, 1960) [Paris: S.E.V.P.E.N., 1960], p. 142.

per man, plus 8 pipes of salt, 1 quintal of oil, 1 quintal of candles, 4 centals (about 400 lbs.) of cod, 2 hogsheads *[barriques]* of sardines and 6 dozen loaves of fresh bread. In January 1547, the *Catherine* of Libourne had a crew of 24 and loaded 1 pipe of biscuit, 1 pipe of wine and 1 side of bacon per man, as much beef as the men could want, 2 *barattes* (churnfulls) of butter, 2 centals of cod, 1 small barrel of vinegar, and 35 butts of salt. In 1548, the following victuals were sent to Pasajes for a Labrador-bound ship: 10 butts of wine, 60 hogsheads of biscuit, 5 small barrels of peas and 1 small barrel of tallow candles. Two years later the *Anthoine* of Saint-Jean-de-Luz sailed for Terranova with 36 butts and 1 hogshead of wine, 20 hogsheads of hake, 10 bales of eel and 40 hogsheads of biscuit.[46]

In addition to the provisions shipped by the outfitter, individual crew members would take their own cheese, high-quality wine, raisins and almonds. All in all, it would appear that the Labrador whalemen were better fed than their compatriots who stayed behind at home — a good incentive to sign onto an expedition!

Loading of victuals would sometimes give rise to disputes and swindles. The records of the Junta of Guipuzcoa show that in the month of April 1575 the outfitter of certain ships leaving for Terranova apparently filled barrels with wood shavings instead of provisions, thus causing the loss of these ships and their crews.[47] It was usually the captain or the outfitter who prepared the list of goods put on board by each of the suppliers. When the ship returned, this document would be used as a reference when sharing out the income from the expedition.

The Crews

Whaling was a matter of team work, and success or failure depended in part on the selection of crew members. The more experienced they were, and the more respected the officers, the greater the chances of a fruitful expedition.

Both the owner and the outfitter were responsible for crew selection. According to a charter contract signed in 1583 between an owner, Sebastian de La Bastida, and three outfitters, Sebastian de Valerdi, Martin de Arostegui and Antonio de Amezti,

46 Jacques Bernard, *Navires et gens..., op. cit.*, p. 812.
47 Mariano Ciriquiain Gaiztarro, *Los Vascos..., op. cit.*, p. 229.

the owner agreed to appoint the master, boatswain, carpenter, caulker, gunner and steward and to pay them. The rest of the crew of 100 was to be chosen and paid by the outfitters.[48] This shows how the owner was able, through intermediaries named by him, to establish his authority or, at any rate, not leave everything up to the captain, who usually represented the outfitters. In some cases, for example the *Trinidad* in 1564, the owner appointed even the captain.[49]

While agreements between owners and outfitters were generally made in writing in the presence of a notary, those between captains and crew members were most often verbal. As a result, we do not have a complete picture of how crews were recruited or of all the conditions of the agreements. One of the rare ones available dates from 1571. It was between Captain Clemente de Agorreta and the coopers Joan de Berrobi and Miguel de Hurbieta. The latter agreed to serve on a whaler belonging to Andres de Alçola in exchange for 19 barrels of oil payable upon the ship's return.[50]

According to the documentary evidence, crews ranged from 50 to 120 men depending on the ship's tonnage.[51] As a rule, there were 25 men per 100 tons,[52] and they were divided into three more or less equal groups: officers and skilled tradesmen, mariners, and apprenticing boys, with a considerable amount of mobility between the three levels. After just a few voyages, an apprentice could easily become an officer or skilled tradesman. The officers — or *oficiales* as they were called at the time — included the captain (who often held shares in the enterprise), master (who looked after the commercial aspect of the expedition and was sometimes the owner of the ship), boatswain, gunner, steward or storesman, barber (i.e. surgeon), and pilot (who might guide several ships simultaneously as a convoy).[53] The skilled tradesmen included the carpenter, caulker, cooper, harpooner and flenser. An examination of the graves at Red Bay reveals that the tradesmen were sturdy and relatively

48 Spain. Valladolid. ARC. Pleitos civiles, Masas fenecidos, box 511-3.

49 The Basque Country. AHPG. Oñate. Partido de Vergara, vol. 2579, reg. 1, fol. 7.

50 The Basque Country. AGDG. Tolosa. Corregimiento de Guipuzcoa, Civiles Elorza, Legajo 216, fol. 64r.

51 Selma Barkham, "Building Materials for Canada in 1556," *Bulletin of the Association for Preservation Technology,* Vol. 5, No. 4 (1973), p. 94.

52 Laurier Turgeon, "Pêches basques...," *op. cit.*, p. 113.

53 The term "officer" must be understood in the meaning it had in Spain at the time. It included, for instance, the *oficial carpintero*, the master carpenter who occupied the "office" of ship's carpenter.

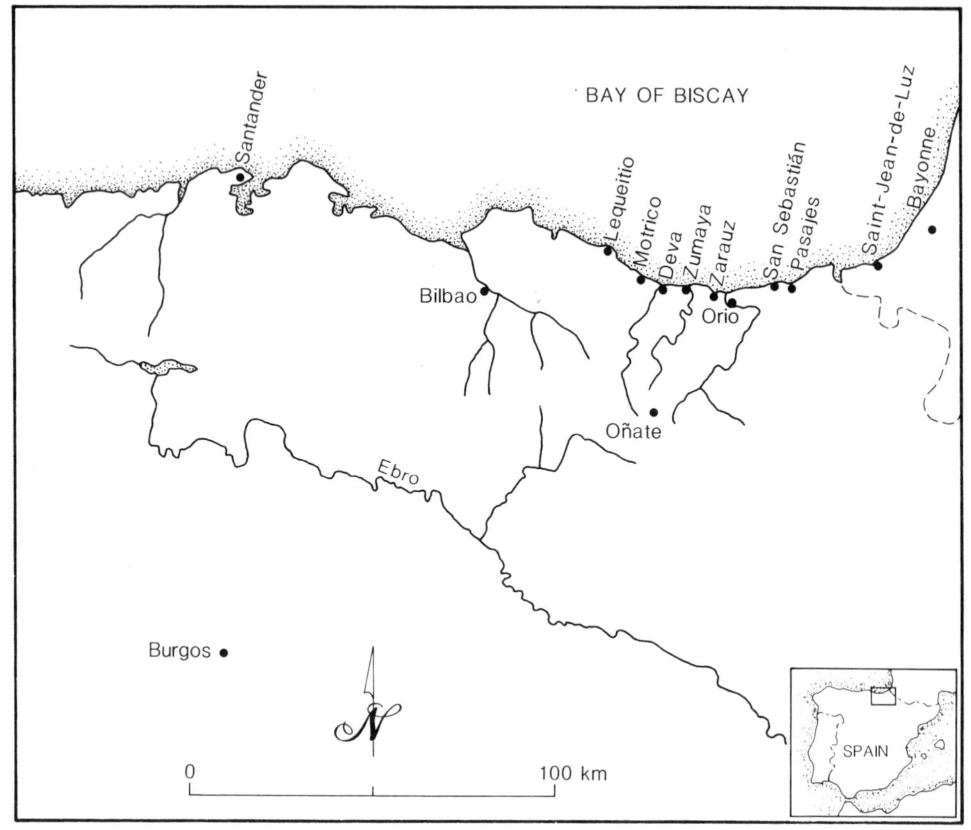

6. The Basque coastline. *Drawing: Dorothea Kappler.*

young. As for the apprentices, there were two groups: those learning to be an officer or tradesman and those learning whale-hunting.[54] Unlike the situation in merchant shipping or even cod fishing, apprentices in the latter group had to be men rather than boys because whaling was such difficult and dangerous work.[55] However those learning a trade like caulker or cooper were generally 11 or 12 years old, and were often the sons or nephews of the ship's tradesmen.

Thus the crew of a 250-ton Basque whaler would typically include a captain, master, boatswain, some coopers, carpenter, possibly a pilot, caulker and gunner, about thirty mariners (from amongst whom the harpooners and flensers were recruited), and about twenty apprentices.[56] Bigger ships would also have a chaplain, a surgeon (who would probably go from port to port caring for the sick and wounded with his ointments, oils, plasters, powders and preserves), a waterboy, a steward, ship's boys, and even a diver to repair the underwater part of the ship.

The crew was hired in late winter and early spring. Each man was responsible for providing, at his own expense, certain essential items such as clothing. Since expeditions were long and often involved great variations in climate, the men needed clothing for all conditions from drought to drenching rain, from heat waves to spells of intense cold. The notarial archives contain dozens and dozens of documents concerning loans made by whalemen to purchase clothing for the trip. Amounts borrowed were between five and 17 ducats, repayable in kind, plus interest of between one-tenth of a share and two shares depending on the amount borrowed.[57] The clothing would include:

– An overgarment, similar to a large cape with sleeves and a hood, made of coarse homespun and lined with fleece, with a nap like English or Irish frieze. It closely resembled the large capes called *kapusai* which Basque shepherds were still

54 The Basque notarial archives contain several apprenticeship contracts. They were generally for a period of two to four years, with the master agreeing to provide his knowledge, tools and sometimes clothing and food in exchange for work and a portion of the wage if applicable. The Basque Country. AHPG. Oñate. Partido de Vergara, Vol. 2578, reg. 2, fol. 29v; reg. 15, fol. 36; Vol. 2580, reg. 2, fol. 16.

55 Jacques Bernard, "Les types de navires...," *op. cit.*, p. 220.

56 A. Arrinda, *Euskalerria eta arrantza* (Donostia Aurrezki Kutxa, 1977), p. 101. Sebastian de la Bastida's ship had five coopers during his 1580 expedition. The Basque Country. AGDG. Tolosa. Corregimiento, Civiles Mandiola, Legajo 424.

57 The Basque Country. AHPG. Oñate. Partido de Vergara, Vol. 2578, reg. 6, fol. 9, 13v; reg. 8, fol. 16, 30, 35; reg. 9, fol. 11v; reg. 12, fol. 17v; reg. 15, fol. 19; Vol. 2579, reg. 1, fol. 14.

wearing in the early 20th century. According to Don Josu Oregui of the Basque Academy, the overgarment was made of raw wool without the natural oils removed so as to provide waterproofing.

- A leather or fur outfit.
- Five to seven linen shirts. Judging from the graves at Red Bay, the whalers also wore wool shirts with long sleeves and a rolled collar.
- Five to seven jackets worn beneath the overgarment, including three of wool, two of coarse cloth, one of hide (sheep or goat, including the hair), and one of canvas. Only the cloth jackets are mentioned as coming in pairs [*pares de vestidos*]; the reference may be to a pant or to some sort of doublet that was to be paired with a jacket. The hide jackets, which are mentioned as single items, might then be a sort of tunic covering the cloth jackets.
- Mariner's breeches extending to just above the knees. The breeches found at Red Bay were of very dark brown serge.
- Two or three metres of fabric to make gaiters to cover the man's legs. The Red Bay graves show that long pants covering the entire leg were sometimes used instead.
- Five or six pairs of blue wool stockings from the Roncal valley in Navarre, probably held up with garters.
- A pair of calf-leather boots.
- Four to six pairs of ankle-high sheep or goat leather slippers.
- Gloves, probably of the same fabric as the gaiters.
- A wool cap.

All of this, together with a blanket and mattress, would be kept in a bag and placed in a small locked barrel or chest.[58]

According to a notarial document signed in Bordeaux on April 26, 1565, certain French cod fishermen were importing material from England to make their clothes

58 Michael Barkham, "*Aspects of life...*," *op. cit.*, p. 33. The archaeologists at Red Bay have exhumed the bodies of two Basque whalemen, one of whom was dressed in pants and a light fabric shirt, and the other in a cap, a shirt, a wool jacket, knee-length breeches, stockings and shoes. James Tuck, "Excavations at Red Bay, Labrador," *Archaeology in Newfoundland and Labrador,* Historic Resources Division, Department of Culture, Recreation & Youth, Government of Newfoundland and Labrador, No. 5 (1984), p. 224-47.

for the voyage. The document speaks of 19 "ells of *cordilhat* from England ... to make clothing."[59] According to Jacques Bernard, the sailors had a definite taste for bright colours, and the result was:

> *a motley display combining red and blue caps and red shirts with black, white or red breeches, tunics with yellow linings, green jerkins and even green breeches, while the sartorial elegance of the ship's master would be enhanced with a triangular hat, a silver chain for his whistle, a doublet, and a sword and purse hanging from his belt.*[60]

A few days before the ship sailed, the crew members would settle their personal affairs either before a notary or by mutual agreement. Given the risks of the crossing, of whaling itself, and of disease, some of them would prepare their wills while others would sign proxies enabling their wives to act in their name while they were away. During the fishing and whaling season in Terranova, there were so few able-bodied men in the Basque country that visiting ships in the ports would often be towed by women.

The Departure and the Crossing

In the 16th century, the Basques were a deeply religious and very superstitious people. When the time came for the ships to leave on a lengthy expedition, a variety of incantations were used to ensure the success of the enterprise. On the day of departure at Lequeitio, tradition called for the crews to take holy water from three different fonts in one church while the clock struck noon. They would then bless their ships with the water.[61] To ensure a successful hunt, the Dominican monks would give the sailors a piece of the robe of the Virgin of the Rosary, and to ward off witches the monks provided St. Peter's wort, which the sailors would burn once on board along with flowers that had been blessed for this purpose.[62] On the day of

59 France. Bordeaux. ADG. Notaire Brigot, 3E2418, fol. 111v. *Cordilhat* or *cordillas* is a coarse woollen material similar to homespun or coarse cloth.

60 Jacques Bernard, *Navires et gens...*, *op. cit.*, p. 622.

61 Mariano Ciriquiain Gaiztarro, *Los Vascos...*, *op. cit.*, p. 9.

62 J.M. Ugartechea y Salinas, *op. cit.*, p. 12. Witchcraft and performance of devotions are known to have played important roles in Basque tradition. They never spoke the words for devil, cat, rat or witch when at sea. According to Pierre de Lancre, Basque sorcery arose from a desire on the part of the women to know what was happening to their husbands during the stay in Terranova!

the departure, a priest would formally bless the sailors and celebrate a special mass on the bow of one of the ships, his face turned toward the stern.[63] At Saint-Jean-de-Luz, the ritual used on this occasion was the one contained in the 1543 Bayonne missal.

The whaling ships generally left for Labrador between mid-June and early July. Leaving any later would not have allowed sufficient time for setting up facilities on the coast before the season began. Some ships left earlier, as in the case of the *Catalina*, whose owner made plans to leave Spain in late March.[64] Such early departures were probably motivated by a desire to fill the holds during the whales' first pass by the Labrador coast in June. Historical records clearly show the existence of two whaling periods in the area, the autumn period being by far the more important.[65]

In the 16th century, few felt any need to keep logs, and as a result we know little about the route taken, navigating techniques or life on board. As regards the route, the records of a trial held in 1572 state that before hitting the open sea, ships leaving San Sebastián and Pasajes would follow the Basque shoreline and stop in the principal ports such as Guetaria [Getaria], Zumaya [Zumaia], Deva [Deba], Motrico [Mutriku] and Lequeitio to take on crew members.[66] Captains or pilots would then choose one of three possible routes. The first continued along the northern shore of Spain toward the Azores, following the trade winds to America, and the Gulf Stream north to Terranova. A more difficult route, because of storms and opposing winds, yet facilitated somewhat by the North Atlantic current, led to Ushant Isle, the Isles of Scilly, Ireland, Scotland, Iceland and then heading west to America. This was the route taken by the Bretons and Normans. Finally, according to an influential official and specialist in shipbuilding named Cristobal de Barros, the Basques followed the northern coast of Spain to Cabo de Peñas, 10 km northwest of Gijon, and from there sailed due WNW at latitude 52°30'N until they reached "The Grand Bay" [the Strait of Belle Isle] 800 leagues from home.[67] Such a route with no stopover may at first

63 Mariano Ciriquiain Gaiztarro, *Los Vascos..., op. cit.,* p. 229.

64 The Basque Country. AGDG. Tolosa. Corregimiento, Ejecutivos Elorza, Legajo 289, fol. 10r.

65 The Basque Country. AGDG. Tolosa. Corregimiento, Civiles Elorza, Legajo 445, "s.fol."

66 The Basque Country. AGDG. Tolosa. Corregimiento, Civiles Elorza, Legajo 216, fol. 57r.

67 Selma Barkham, "Los Vascos y las pesquerias transatlanticas: 1517-1713," in *Itsasoa 3,* edited by Enrique Ayerbe (1988), p. 58.

seem surprising, but modern transatlantic shipping shows that it is possible if there are favourable winds from the east, north and southwest.

Navigation in the 16th century was based on guesswork despite the existence since the late Middle Ages of instruments such as the log, compass, hourglass, astrolabe, Jacob's staff, and sounding line. Most of these were imprecise and only worked properly on land. For example, the magnetic declination would vary depending on where the compass had been made. Thus navigators could not tell exactly where they were when at sea, either in terms of latitude or in terms of longitude. Nautical science at this time consisted of pilots' experience and their skill in observing the position of the sun and stars, the direction of the winds and currents, the motions of the sea, the presence of cumulus clouds, changes in the colour of the water, and fish and birds peculiar to specific regions. These would enable a pilot to determine with some degree of accuracy how much time had elapsed and the location of the ship. In recounting a voyage in 1573, Eugenio de Salazar made clear his scepticism about the ability of pilots when he wrote sarcastically: "Ah! How well God reveals his supreme power when he entrusts the subtle and vital art of navigation to the obtuse decisions and coarse hands of pilots."[68] In short, navigation was not a science but an art, an art that was severely tested during storms. Whalers took the precaution of including in their accounts a sum of money set aside specifically for pilgrimages which the sailors promised to make in exchange for a favour. One such favour was escape from storms.

During the 16th century, an Atlantic crossing typically took two months.[69] Historian Michael Lewis has described the conditions on board English ships in Tudor times, and conditions must have been similar (or worse) on whalers. It is clear that the ships were uncomfortable. Only rarely did the captain have a bed in a small cabin on the poop (described ironically by the poet Eustache Deschamps as the ship's "main palace").[70] The men slept in pairs using the same straw mattress, which was laid out under the cuddy at the forward end, in the bridge house or under the open sky. They slept fully dressed, in clothes that were sometimes wet. The air was putrid

68 Cesareo Fernandez Duro, *op. cit.,* Vol. 2, p. 198.

69 The average speed of 16th-century ships is thought to have been 3 or 4 knots an hour. Patrick Pomey, "Comment naviguait-on dnas la Méditerrannée romaine?" *L'Histoire,* No. 36 (July-August 1981), p. 101.

70 Michel Mollat, *La vie quotidienne des gens de mer en Atlantique: IXe - XVIe siècle* (Paris: Hachette, 1983), p. 147.

and dank, the moisture spoiling everything that was prone to spoilage. The sailors did not bathe because there was not enough fresh water. They did not clean the ship either, so it was revoltingly filthy. Accumulated refuse filtered down from the upper decks, creating a good environment for disease to spread. Drinking water was too precious to use for anything but drinking, and it stood stagnating in barrels waiting to be consumed. As to the food, it was often in a rather pitiful condition when it was loaded, and by the time it was consumed it was sometimes rotten.[71] Once food had become totally inedible, the crew would protest and refuse to eat it, and it would be thrown overboard. But once supplies began to run out, the men were obliged to eat whatever was in the barrels down to the last scraps, no matter how repulsive it might be, using salt or spices to mask the taste. In his telling of a trip to Brazil, Jean de Léry mentions that

> *the rain had spoiled the biscuit, yet we had not only to eat it in its rotten state, but also, on pain of starving to death, we could not throw any part of it away and so we ate worms that were as numerous as the crumbs we made while we ate. And our fresh water was so corrupted, and likewise so full of worms ... that none could refrain from spitting it out, and so the cup was held in one hand while the nose was held with the other to avoid the stink.*[72]

Toilets were non-existent. Weather permitting, the men would use the ship's latrines, which projected from either side of the stem, using a length of tarred rope as toilet paper.

Yet we must avoid overgeneralizing. Despite the often deplorable conditions, men accustomed to life at sea would have recognized the benefits of elementary hygiene and they must have attempted to comply as much as possible with orders by occasionally washing the ship down using vinegar as a disinfectant, and getting rid of refuse. Also conditions might vary somewhat depending on the destination and on which country had outfitted the ship. Clearly the fresh air of Labrador was more conducive to good health and food preservation than the hot, humid climate of the south. A final point here is that shipboard conditions were really not much different from

71 The English had a saying "God sends food and the devil cooks it." Michel Mollat, *op. cit.*, p. 147.

72 Jean de Léry, *Histoire d'un voyage fait en la terre du Brésil* (Lausanne: Bibliothèque romande, 1972), p. 53

those the sailors were familiar with at home, so the cramped and often insalubrious spaces on board ship were not necessarily disorienting for them.

During the crossing, each member of the crew had his own responsibilities, as described by Diego Garcia de Palacio, the author of a well-known treatise on shipbuilding dating from the late 16th century.[73] The captain was the supreme authority.[74] He was responsible for discipline and supervised all operations and manoeuvres related to navigation or to the upkeep of the ship and its cargo. He had to be strict and demanding, but fair. Second in rank was the master, who was responsible for the commercial aspect of the voyage. He had to have a good knowledge of how to load and stow goods, buy all necessities for the ship, report on this in writing to the captain and check that the ship was in good condition.

The pilot had to have extensive experience and understand the workings of navigating instruments. His essential tools included marine charts, dividers, a twelve-pound astrolabe to measure the height of the sun, a Jacob's staff or cross staff with scales of 60 to 20 degrees and 20 to 8 degrees, a wooden quadrant to determine latitude, two marine clocks from Lisbon, two compasses, two Venetian hourglasses, one copper lantern, cotton for wicks and 100 fathoms of tarred oakum with six pounds of lead for the sounding line. The pilot's particular concern was the tiller and the foremast, these being the most vital to steering the ship.

The boatswain kept a record of all goods loaded on board the vessel and saw that they were properly stowed, with light and valuable articles being placed on top of the rest of the cargo and far from the bow, the stern and the hatchway. He also had to ensure that the cordage was in good condition, extinguish the firebox and lanterns every night, check the condition of the pump, batten the hatch, transmit the pilot's orders with a whistle and organize the watches. The boatswain's mate was responsible for the ship's boys and the apprentices, and he assisted the boatswain in all of the latter's duties.

The steward was responsible for the stores of food and drink and their distribution at mealtimes. Breakfast was eaten standing and consisted of a ration of biscuit, a few cloves of garlic, sardine or cheese and some wine. Meat was served only on

73 Diego Garcia de Palacio, *Nautical instruction, 1587* (Bisbee: Terrenate Association, 1986), p. 139-47.

74 In a fairly unusual case in 1565, Francisco de Narruondo and Joanes de Arburu were co-captains of a whaler belonging to Francisco Elorriaga. The Basque Country. AGDG. Tolosa. Corregimiento, Civiles Elorza, Legajo 345, fol. 11r.

Thursdays and Sundays, fish and beans on other days. For the main meals, a table was set up on the deck. On it was placed a ration of ship's biscuit along with four pounds of meat for each group of four men. Each crew member was entitled to three rations of wine or cider. On fish days, the steward would serve each man four sardines per meal, with its own oil and some vinegar. After the men had finished, the apprentices would clear the table and take their turn. They were entitled to the same rations as the sailors except that they were limited to a single ration of wine or cider. The steward was responsible for seeing that they recited the evening prayers and said the "good day" in the morning.

The carpenter had to be able to make any necessary repairs to the ship or the boats it carried, and he had to have all the tools needed for this purpose. The caulker was responsible for the pump. He kept the ship fully sealed and to do this he had the ship's boys make oakum out of old cord. The ship's doctor had to have all medications needed to cure illnesses and take care of the most common types of injury. The mariners needed to know how to manipulate the sails, secure the cargo, steer a boat and weigh anchor. They were normally divided into two groups that took turns on the four-hour watches. The ship's boys had to be able to climb the masts, row, operate the pump and lower the boats. Those who didn't know how learned quickly enough with the help of a few strokes of a ratline! As to the ship's boys some were assigned specifically to serve the captain, master and pilot,[75] while the others had to clean the ship, set the table, serve meals and drinks and recite prayers. They had to obey orders promptly. In one case, a boatswain's mate assigned seven of them to sweep the bridge but gave them only six brooms. When the order to sweep was given, the seven ran towards the brooms but inevitably one of them ended up empty-handed. To punish him for his lack of diligence, the officer ordered three lashes.[76]

Setting up on the Labrador Coast

Upon arrival in Terranova, the captain's first task was to find a well-protected harbour where a whaling station could be set up. Unfortunately we do not know what

75 The Basque Country. AGDG. Tolosa. Corregimiento, Civiles Lecuona, Legajo 9, file 203, fol. 143r.

76 Cesareo Fernandez Duro, *op. cit.*, Vol. 5, p. 475, note 1.

criteria the Basques used to select a location. Certainly they must have given consideration to accessibility to the sea, intensity and direction of currents, depth of the water, ship safety, and protection from the weather and from the native peoples. Many of the harbours used by the Basques in Labrador have one geographical feature in common: the presence of an island in the middle of the bay. This was probably motivated by considerations of safety and security. Once a site had been selected by a given group of whalemen, they would return there each year for several years. This is at any rate the logical conclusion to be drawn from the information in certain notarial documents to the effect that when the season was over, the crew would often leave boats and equipment — presumably for use the following year.

There are no descriptions of the various tasks carried out by Basque crews during setup on the Labrador coast. However one early 18th-century historian, Zorgdrager, has given a faithful description of how the Dutch set up their stations on Spitsbergen around 1620, half a century after the period of Basque whaling in Labrador.[77] In view of the fact that the Dutch learned whaling from the Basques, and that the geographical environment of Labrador is much like that of Spitsbergen, we are justified in extrapolating from one case to the other.

Upon entering the harbour, the captain's first duty was to find a place to moor the ship.[78] The location had to be both safe and functional, that is, near the "ovens," so that the barrels of oil could be loaded without too much effort. According to the Dutch description, an anchor was dropped at the bow of the ship and the stern was secured by a solid line to some protruding object on the shore — a large rock, the base of an oven, or a deposit of bones from previously killed whales.[79] Once the ship was moored, it was used as living quarters, as a place to store equipment and whale oil, and during flensing operations. It is therefore probable that the rigging was taken

77 James Travis Jenkins, *A History of the Whale Fisheries* (London: H.F. & G. Witherby, 1921), p. 127.

78 This is confirmed by Champlain, who writes that the Basques "put their vessels in a safe port, or near one, in a place where they believe there to be a good quantity of whales, and they outfit several shallops manned by good men." C.H. Laverdière (ed.), *Oeuvres de Champlain* (Québec: Université Laval, 1870), Vol. 1, p. 374. According to other sources, it would appear that the whaling ship was itself actively involved in the hunt. Thus it seems that the *Maria* was shipwrecked in 1572 while engaged in the chase. Selma Barkham, "Documentary evidence...," *op. cit.*, p. 75.

79 During a storm in 1565, the crew of the *Santo Crucifixo de Burgos* had to cut the lines by which the ship was attached to the shore. This shows that the vessel was moored in the harbour. The Basque Country. AGDG. Tolosa. Corregimiento, Civiles Elorza, Legajo 213.

down. When more than one ship anchored in the same harbour, as often happened in Labrador, and specifically at Red Bay, they would be positioned in tight rows one behind the other, just far enough apart to allow for the boats bringing the barrels of oil from shore.[80]

The next step was to erect the on-shore facilities. Once again, we have no precise and detailed description of the work this involved. However it is possible to make a few deductions from scraps of documentary information — deductions which have now been confirmed by the archaeological excavations at Red Bay. We now know that one of the first tasks of the carpenters was to construct and repair the *cabañas* or shelters that were used for rendering the blubber into oil.[81] The documents reveal that the Basques took nails, clay and tiles with them for this purpose, and that they built on sloping terrain just as they did in Europe. First they erected a low wall facing a steep rocky outcropping. The wall was used as a base for tree trunks that served as pillars. On this framework they then placed rafters, with one end resting on the pillars and the other on the rock. One historian mentions that the rafters were then covered with baleen plates (whalebone) to support the roofing tiles.[82] These thin tiles were waterproof, light and durable. They were also very poor conductors of heat and the cheapest roofing material available at the time. Archaeologists from Memorial University have discovered an 14 metre by 8 metre area at Red Bay completely covered with such tiles. It is thought that they were the roof of a structure of slightly smaller dimensions.[83] The two end walls, if they ever existed, have left no trace, whereas a line of cobbles is still visible showing where the front wall was. The numerous tools and pieces of pottery found inside the walls suggest that it was a workshop.

The carpenter also had to build housing for the coopers. Unlike in Spitsbergen, where a good portion of the crew lived on land in stone buildings covered with

80 James Travis Jenkins, *op. cit.*, p. 127. This practice is confirmed by a document according to which the ships owned by Joanes de Galarraga and Domingo de Oloscoaga were anchored one next to the other (*una cabe*) in the port of St. Augustin [Canada Pequeña] in 1580. The Basque Country. AGDG. Tolosa, Corregimiento, Civiles Mandiola, Legajo 424, fol. 34v.

81 One document tells us that in 1564, Francisco de Janregueta and Simon de Azcoitia had a conversation in the port of Sonbrero "junto a la cabana que tenyan fecha para el derretir de las ballenas" (beside the cabin they had made for the boiling down of the whales). The Basque Country. AGDG. Tolosa. Corregimiento, Civiles Elorza, Legajo 65, fol. 24v.

82 Iñaki Zumalde, *op. cit.*, 30 March 1980, p. 6.

83 James Tuck and Robert Grenier, "A 16th-Century Basque Whaling Station in Labrador," *Scientific American*, Vol. 245, No. 5 (November 1981), p. 183.

planking, in Labrador only the coopers were housed on shore, while the other crew members slept on board ship.[84] Archaeological work at Red Bay has not yet revealed any definite case of a dwelling structure on shore other than the coopers' workshops and residences. Also, a will written in Labrador in 1584 specifies that at the time of writing it was midnight and some of the whalemen were at work rendering whale blubber while the others were sleeping on board the ship.[85]

While the carpenter was at work at these various tasks, the coopers had to assemble the parts of the barrels, which had been transported in knocked-down form to save space. [86] Meanwhile, members of the crew were probably busy installing the cauldrons on the ovens or else cutting wood. Once all this was done the hunt could begin.

The Method of Capture

The first step was to find one or more whales. So far, the archaeologists at Red Bay have not found definite proof of the existence of lookout towers similar to those used a few centuries earlier along the Basque coast. Of course, this does not prove that no such towers existed: over the years the region's severe climate would have destroyed such makeshift structures, exposed as they were at the tops of rocky outcroppings.

Champlain states that in order to sight a whale, the Basques would send a shallop out from the harbour and "it would patrol back and forth."[87] This is corroborated by the evidence of captain Juan Lopez de Reçu at a trial in 1575, who stated that after he arrived at Red Bay he had sent some members of his crew to search for whales in boats belonging to his ship.[88] This approach would certainly seem to be as suited to conditions in the Strait of Belle Isle as the lookout tower method, which might not be so effective because of the frequent fog in the region. Given the narrowness of the

84 James Travis Jenkins, *op. cit.,* p. 85. Spain. Valladolid. ARC. Pleitos civiles, Legajo 54, box 312-1.

85 The Basque Country. AHPG. Oñate. Partido de San Sebastian, Legajo 1808, fol. 44s.

86 On the technology of 16th-century Basque barrel-making and how the parts were assembled, see Lester A. Ross, "Sixteenth-century Spanish Basque Coopering Technology: A Report on the Staved Containers Found in 1978-79 on the Wreck of the Whaling Galleon *San Juan,* sunk in Red Bay, Labrador, AD 1565," Manuscript Report Series No. 408, (Ottawa: Parks Canada, 1980).

87 C.H. Laverdière, *op. cit.,* Vol. 1, p. 375. This method certainly implies that there were very large numbers of whales along the coast.

88 Spain. Valladolid. ARC. Pleitos civiles, Legajo 54, box 312-1.

Strait, a few well-placed whaleboats could easily monitor it. The boats were possibly permanently anchored along the coast, fully equipped for whaling.

Once the whale was sighted, the whaleboats would set out in pursuit. Several pieces of testimony at a trial suggest that these six-man shallops might belong to more than one whaling ship.[89] It is inconceivable that the crews of four or five independent whalers would fight amongst themselves for the whales. This would have meant a duplication of tasks and costs, as well as quarrels and pitched battles among the whalemen. An agreement among four captains anchored in the port of Canada Pequeña [St. Augustin], in 1580, which was later the subject of a trial, describes in considerable detail the sort of association that might arise among different ships on such occasions.[90] According to the trial records, the contracting parties drew lots for all the captured whales which yielded more than 40 barrels of oil. When a captain won, his name would be struck from the list, until chance had done its work and each ship had received its share. The smaller whales, those yielding less than 40 barrels, constituted a sort of common kitty that was shared among all members of the association on the basis of the size of each ship's crew. There must also have been a similar tacit agreement governing the work of sighting, chasing, capturing and flensing the whales and trying their blubber. There may even have been an agreement about obtaining provisions of local supplies.

The boats chased the whales as silently as possible, under sail or oar power. To dampen noise, the oarlocks were lined with braided hempcord and coated with tallow. All the men rowed including the harpooner at the front. First they had to position the shallop between the whale and the open sea so as to force it toward the shore. Then they approached it from the rear at an angle, in order to take maximum advantage of the blind spot in the animal's field of vision. Once they were near the whale, the helmsman (who was the officer in command) would order the harpooner to stand up so as to be able to assist in guiding the boat into a good position. The harpooner would convey the direction to take by gestures made with his hand behind his back. At the same time, he would secure his oar handle in the hole in the cleat at his feet, take the harpoons and lances from under the thwarts and place them in a support located at the front of the boat. Once the boat was within seven or eight metres of the

89 Idem.

90 The Basque Country. AGDG. Tolosa. Corregimiento, Civiles Mandiolla, Legajo 424.

whale, the harpooner would support himself by placing his left leg in the half-moon notch in the cuddy board and his right leg against his seat. He would seize the first harpoon and propel it with one or both hands into the animal's body, taking care to avoid the head, which was too bony. Sometimes the boat would be close enough that the harpooner could use his shoulder, and hence his own weight, to ram the harpoon even deeper. The purpose of the harpoon was not to kill the whale but to connect the men to their quarry in such a way that it could not escape. Some writers note that the harpooner would throw a second harpoon if he had time. We do not know whether this method was in use in Labrador in the 16th century, or whether it was a 17th-century innovation. Nor do we know the purpose of the second harpoon. Some claim that a wooden buoy of one square metre was attached to it so that the whale could be spotted again if it succeeded in freeing itself from the first harpoon, or if the cord of the first harpoon had to be cut.[91] Others claim that the second harpoon was connected to the cord of the first harpoon by a slipknot and that its sole purpose was to increase the chances of capturing the whale if the animal managed to get free of the first harpoon.[92] If this is true, then in cases where the harpooner did not have time to secure the backup harpoon in the whale's body, he would have had to throw it into the sea as quickly as possible to avoid serious injury to crew members or to prevent the boat from capsizing.

When the whale felt the harpoon penetrate its flesh, it would either dive or swim away very quickly along the water's surface. As it did so, it would drag along the whaleline, which had to unwind freely if serious injury or capsizing were to be avoided. There are many examples of whalemen being pulled into the water when the line became wound around their ankles or wrists. Thus the oars had to be positioned on the side of the boat in such a way as not to obstruct the motion of the line down the centre. The line would unwind so rapidly that the crew members watching it had to keep it wet so that it would not burst into flames when it touched the groove in the stem. Meanwhile the steerer would be working in the rear to prevent the boat from capsizing, by keeping its lengthwise axis in line with the rope. Champlain states that the whale would sometimes drag the boat "more than eight or nine leagues, moving as fast as a horse."[93] Now if the line was fastened to the bow

91 Antonio Sañez Reguart, *op. cit.,* p 380.

92 A. Arrinda, *op. cit.,* p. 161 and René Bélanger, *op. cit.* p. 126.

93 C.H. Laverdière, *op. cit.,* Vol. 1, p. 376.

thwart, and the whale dived deep enough to use up the 300 metres of line, then it would have been necessary to sever the line with an axe to prevent the boat and crew from being dragged under the water.[94] However, none of the bitts generally associated with this technique have been found in the shallops discovered at Red Bay. That does not mean the Basques did not use this method, but in the current state of our knowledge, we must conclude that the end of the rope was connected to some sort of buoy that allowed the men to keep the whale in sight at all times.

Usually the whale would calm down and return to the surface to breathe before the second, standby line was used up. The whalers would then pull on the line to bring themselves to a position near the quarry. All that remained was to kill the animal. This was done with the lance, which the harpooner would sink into the whale's body, aiming for the vital parts such as the heart or lungs. If he had time, he would withdraw the lance and strike a second time. This was a dangerous moment. In a final burst of energy, the whale might capsize the boat with a single movement of its tail. To reduce this danger, the men would sometimes cut the tendons in the whale's tail.

After a few minutes of struggle, the whale would finally be still. As it tired from loss of blood its movements would slow down. The blood would spurt less forcefully from its vents. The end was near. In a final effort, the whale would beat the blood-reddened sea with its tail one last time before dying. Then all that remained was to tow the quarry ashore, an operation that could take several hours depending on the winds and currents. If it appeared that the carcass was going to sink, boats would be positioned on either side of it connected by a sturdy rope passing under the body, or it would be attached by the tail using a slipknot.[95] Our documents state the need for at least two boats for this purpose.[96] If winds and currents were unfavourable, the whale might be anchored temporarily in a small cove, but this created another sort of

---

94 This technique was later perfected: rather than tying the end of the line to the boat, a loop was added to which a fresh coil of rope could be attached if necessary. A simple signal would be given to attract other boats, which would assist by bringing their own lines. It is hard to imagine that both techniques were in use at the same period of time, as Maxime Dégros asserts. Maxime Dégros, *op. cit.*, No. 43 (1943), p. 56.

95 Some authors, probably basing themselves on the account by John Monck written in Spitsbergen in 1620, believe that the boats would tow the whale to the ship, which would then take it to land. This would imply that the whaling ship took an active part in the hunt. This was not the case in the 16th-century whalehunt in Labrador, where whales were abundant near the shore. A. Arrinda, *op. cit.*, p. 147.

96 Spain. Valladolid. ARC. Pleitos civiles, Legajo 54, box 312-1.

7. A Basque whaleboat being unloaded. *Drawing: Richard Schlecht, © 1985 National Geographical Society.*

8. Blubber is flensed from a whale, cut into smaller blocks on the platform and then rendered into oil in the ovens under the tile roof. *Drawing: Richard Schlecht. © 1985 National Geographical Society.*

risk. Captain Juan Lopez de Reçu's crew had been forced to abandon a whale in the small bay of Antongoçulo because of bad weather. When they returned a few days later, they found that whalemen from another ship anchored in a nearby harbour had made off with their catch.[97]

With the whale secure, it was time for the men to give thanks to God for protecting them and assisting their victory. The Basques were deeply religious and had a prayer for every aspect of a whaling expedition. The prayer of thanks read as follows:

> *Receive, O Lord, our thanks and our praise a millionfold and a billionfold for in Thy generosity Thou hast done us the favour of taking the life of this the greatest of fishes. Compared to his strength, our strength was nothing. We felt Thy favour during the struggle. Thanks to Thee, we have vanquished this colossus of the seas, we have dragged it to land covered with its wounds and we have stripped it, where before it was a ferocious beast that tossed about in the seas indomitable, a miracle of nature. Honour and thanks to Thee, O Lord.*[98]

The English merchant and colonizer Richard Whitbourne asserts that during the capture, as well as during subsequent procedures, he had seen native people working with the Basques in exchange for a little cider or a piece of bread.[99] The natives are also reported to have done hunting and trading work for the Europeans.[100]

Flensing the Whale and Trying the Blubber

There are two views on the subject of where the flensing work was done. According to the first, the whale was hoisted directly onto shore to be cut up. The men with the aid of a winch hauled the carcass as far as possible onto land. This method, probably in use along the Basque coast in Europe, is illustrated in several works on whaling.[101]

97 *Idem.*

98 René Bélanger, *op. cit.*, p. 114.

99 Iñaki Zumalde, *op. cit.*, Feb. 24, 1980, p. 4.

100 Laurier Turgeon, "Pêches basques...," *op. cit.*, p. 62.

101 Mariano Ciriquiain Gaiztarro, *Los Vascos..., op. cit.;* Antonio Sañez Reguart, *op. cit.;* Rafael Gonzalez Echegaray, *op. cit.*

According to the second view, which is more likely to be correct, the whale was first towed to the ship anchored in the harbour. The body was secured along the length of the hull and the men removed large strips or slabs of blubber, which were then towed ashore. Fotherby gives a description of this method as used in Spitsbergen in 1613:

> *and with their shallops they [the men] towe him to the ships, with his taile foremost; and then they fasten him to the sterne of some ship appointed for that purpose, where he is cutte up in manner as followeth: Two or three men came in a boate, or shallop, to the side of the whale; one man holding the boat close to the whale with a boat-hook, and another who stands either in the boat or upon the whale cutts and scores the fatt, which we call blubber, in square-like pieces, 3 or 4 feet long, with a great cutting-knife. Then, to raise it from the flesh, ther is a crab, or capstowe sett purposely upon the poop of the ship, from whence ther descends a rope, with an iron hook in the end of it; and this hook is made to take fast hould of a piece of the fatt, or blubber: and as, by touring the capstowe, it is raised and lifted up, the cutter with his long knife, looseth it from the flesh, even as if the larde of a swine were, it is in this manner cleane cut off, then doe they lower the capstowe, and lett it downe to float upon the water, makeing a hold in some side or corner of it, whereby they fasten it upon a rope. And so they proceed to cut off more peeces; makeing fast together 10 or twelve of them at once, to be towed ashoare, at the sterne of a boat or shallop.*[102]

In the lists of goods loaded on board whaling ships bound for Labrador, there are several mentions of belts that might have been used for flensing alongside the ship' hull.[103] At a trial held in 1575, a witness speaks of whales that were moored to the *na* and rotated with the aid of the great capstan so that the baleen plates could b removed.[104]

102 Martin W. Conway, *No Man's Land: A History of Spitsbergen from its Discovery in 1596 to the Beginning of the Scientific Explorations of the Country* (Cambridge: Cambridge University Press, 1906), p. 85.

103 Michael Barkham, *Aspects of life..., op. cit.*, p. 29.

104 The Basque Country. AGDG. Tolosa. Corregimientos, Civiles Lecuona, Legajo 9, file 203, fol. 147. This method is also mentioned in a 1580 document: The Basque Country. AGDG. Tolosa. Corregimiento, Civiles Mandiola, Legajo 424, fol. 42v.

On the other hand, the divers at the Red Bay digging site have discovered, in shallow water opposite the ovens, the remains of an inclined surface which could have been used for flensing.[105] Nearby excavations turned up numerous pieces of metal that could be the remains of broken tools. Also, the inclined surface seems to be connected to the ovens by a paved pathway. The divers have also discovered bone deposits very near the shore, which suggests that the flensing work was performed at that location. This might lead to the conclusion that the Basques used a mixed method of flensing: they towed the whales to the ship to remove the upper jaw (containing the baleen plates) with the assistance of the capstan and the rigging pulleys; then they took the rest of the carcass ashore to remove the blubber.

Given the geographical conditions and the technology of the time, it is more logical to conclude that the Basques would have preferred working alongside the ship. It would be easier to flense the animal there than on shore. The carcass could be kept afloat with leather straps or cables attached to the rigging, and it could be turned around to remove the blubber from all sides. On shore, it would call for great mechanical efforts to move the carcass, which weighed many tons. Also, if the work were done alongside the ship, the carcass could simply be left to sink once the blubber had been removed. If the work were done on shore, the skeleton would first have to be towed out into deeper water so that there would be room for the next carcass. Regarding the inclined surfaces, the most plausible hypothesis is that they were used to hoist the long strips of blubber onto the shore after they had been removed from the carcass next to the ship.

The flensing work had to be done quickly or else much less oil would be obtained.[106] The first step was to remove a strip of blubber called the envelope, which extended right around the circumference of the animal's body at the location of the eyes. The next strips were cut off horizontally, i.e. lengthwise along the animal's body from the envelope to the tail. For this purpose a variety of special knives, hooks and hatchets were used. The historian Antonio Sañez Reguart describes several of the tools used for flensing alongside the ship.[107] The handles were extremely long so that the men could work without climbing down onto the carcass. The flensing tools used on land must have been essentially the same, but with shorter handles.

---

105 James A. Tuck and Robert Grenier, *op. cit.*, p. 186.

106 The Basque Country. AGDG. Tolosa. Corregimientos, Civiles Lecuona, Legajo 9, file 203, fol. 38v.

107 Antonio Sañez Reguart, *op. cit.*, p. 148.

The next step was that of trying the blubber, a lengthy and arduous task. The men worked continuously, not stopping until all of the blubber had been processed. Sometimes they had to work into the night hours, as mentioned by Domingo de Miranda when attesting to the validity of the will written by Joanes de Echaniz in Labrador in 1584.[108] First the big strips of blubber were cut into smaller chunks. Numerous knife markings found on the fins suggest that these parts of the whale were used as chopping tools. Chunks of about 20 cm in length were loaded onto handbarrows and taken to the ovens. These were granite and sandstone structures about one metre high by 2.5 metres deep, on which were placed the cast-iron or copper cauldrons.[109] The base of the oven had an opening where fuel could be inserted in the firebox, which was always located on the seaward side. The top had up to six circular openings for the cauldrons. The excavations at Red Bay have revealed the presence of a wooden platform that was erected in front of the ovens for the men to stand on, and it seems likely that the work area as a whole was covered with a roof of tile laid over baleen plates.

Fuel for the ovens consisted of charcoal, bits and pieces from shallops and barrels, or local wood. After lighting the fire, the men would toss the chunks of blubber into the cauldrons using iron pitchforks. The heat would soon turn the blubber to oil. Burnt residues floating at the top would be removed with a skimmer and used as fuel. The operation thus became self-sustaining; indeed, Basque sources claim that these residues burnt better than wood. As the level of oil in the cauldron rose, the men would ladle it out into a nearby tank containing cold water. They had to take care not to leave the cauldron completely empty, because if they did, then newly added chunks of blubber would not melt as quickly. This precaution also added as much as four years to the cauldron's useful life. The water in the tank served to cool the oil and purify it. The oil being less dense than the water, it would float at the surface while the dross would sink.[110] Once cooled, the oil would take on its characteristic colour. If it was too pale, it had to be reheated at high heat, while if it was yellow, it had to be reheated over a low fire. It was then poured through a strainer and into 182-kg barrels, typically 8

108 Selma Barkham, Documentary evidence..., *op. cit.*, p. 85.

109 A. Arrinda, *op. cit.*, p. 80.

110 In Spitsbergen, a boat that was not seaworthy but still waterproof was sometimes used instead of a tank. James A. Tuck and Robert Grenier, *op. cit.*, p. 186.

cm high and 69 cm in diameter at the widest part, with a capacity of 211 litres of oil.[111]

It took two and half days to cut up the whale, try the blubber and stow the oil. Two teams of workers, a night-team on the ship and a day-team on land, would alternate until the job was done. This, at any rate, is the picture that emerges from the one document we have on the subject.[112]

Stowing the Oil

The barrels were probably loaded on board ship as they were filled. The ship's hold would certainly have afforded the best protection against bad weather or other problems that might damage the barrels or cause the oil to deteriorate. True, a sudden wind could sink a ship and its cargo, as happened to the *San Juan* in 1565, but such occurrences were rare. In Spitsbergen, the first step in the stowing operation was to roll the barrels to the shoreline. From there, boats would tow them to the ship. They were then hoisted aboard with block and tackle and lowered into the hold using a canthook. The barrels were stacked four high using stowing-wedges, with the bottom ones lying on the floor of the hold. In the three upper layers, each barrel rested in the hollow formed by four barrels in the layer beneath. Thus each layer was set back with respect to the layer below it. This method made maximum use of the available space. Ballast stones and pieces of wood were scattered about to help keep the cargo in place. The hold of a 350-ton ship could take about 1250 barrels full of oil.

---

111 Lope Martinez de Isasti, *op. cit.*, p. 156. The figures on the capacity of the barrels vary considerably. James A. Tuck and Robert Grenier, *op. cit.*, p. 190, gives 54 gallons; René Cuzacq, *Les Basques chasseurs..., op. cit.*, p. 12, gives 120 to 130 quarts; Camino y Orella, in Mariano Ciriquiain Gaiztarro, *Los Vascos..., op. cit.*, p. 156, gives 100 *azumbres* or 201.6 litres. According to an ordinance issued by Philip II on February 23, 1576, barrels were to weigh 400 pounds, and each village that produced barrels was to place a scale in a public place to ensure compliance with this figure. Mariano Ciriquiain Gaiztarro, *Los Vascos..., op. cit.*, p. 151. The fact that the king issued the ordinance is good evidence that the situation at the time was indeed confused, with numerous differences in container capacity. Note that the Basques sold whale oil by weight, not by measures of liquid volume.

112 Spain. Valladolid. ARC. Pleitos civiles, Legajo 54, box 312-1.

The Return Journey

Historical documents describe voyages during which the crew voluntarily overwintered in Terranova so that they could fill the ship's hold. Such was the case with the voyage of Juanes de Arano's *Catalina* in 1596.[113] On January 19, 1572, Dominica de Aya affirmed that her husband Juan de Berrobi could not testify because he was still in Terranova.[114] But such court cases were rare. As autumn drew to a close and ice started to form on the rivers and ponds, the men would begin preparations for the return journey.[115] If the hunt had been so successful that the ship could not carry all the oil, the captain might ask another ship to carry some of it in exchange for half the number of barrels involved. The amount of space available after loading probably also dictated how many boats the captain would decide to leave behind hidden in caches on the coast.[116] One document even mentions whales left on the shore in anticipation of the next season.[117]

Not much is known about the return trip. One theory suggests that in the 16th century all the ships would congregate at Canso before starting the crossing.[118] From there they would head directly for Cape Finisterre, the trip typically taking 35 to 4[illegible] days. One witness at a trial held in 1566 mentions that his ship had been damaged on December 6 in a storm at 50° north latitude during the return journey.[119]

The arrival of the whaling ships was eagerly awaited in each of the small ports along the Basque coast. The inhabitants would mount a continuous watch, and the first person to spot a ship would receive a monetary reward. Going by the account books, it would also appear that a mass was said on the day a ship returned, to thank God for the success of the expedition, or simply for the safe return of the men.[120] As Sancho Panza put it so well: "If you want to learn to pray, go to sea!"

---

113 The Basque Country. AGDG. Tolosa. Corregimiento, Civiles Lecuona, Legajo 9, file 203, fol. 53v.

114 The Basque Country. AGDG. Tolosa. Corregimiento, Civiles Elorza, Legajo 216, fol. 4r.

115 On the basis of Champlain's writings, René Bélanger claims that the return journey began in early September. René Bélanger, *op. cit.*, p. 31. In James I's grant to Francis Bacon in 1610, it is very clearly stated that the Basques were in the habit of staying in the New Land until December. D.W. Prowse, *A History of Newfoundland from English Colonial and Foreign Records* (London: Eyre & Spotiswoode, 1896), p. 95.

116 The Basque Country. AGDG. Tolosa. Corregimiento, Civiles Elorza, Legajo 37, fol. 17r; Legajo 65 fol. 14r.

117 Spain. Valladolid. ARC. Pleitos civiles, Legajo 54, box 312-1.

118 A. Arrinda, *op. cit.*, p. 159.

119 Spain. Valladolid. ARC. Pleitos civiles, Masas fenecidos 260, box 1045-1.

120 Mariano Ciriquiain Gaiztarro, *Los Vascos...*, *op. cit.*, p. 230.

Chapter III
Whaling in the Basque Economy

It would be presumptuous to attempt to determine the economic significance of Basque whaling with the research data available today. To do this, we would need a greater number and a wider variety of the notarial documents which constitute the sole source of information about the whaling trade in the 16th century. And even if we had them, there is no guarantee that the results would be more significant, because in the first place, these documents do not allow us to establish conclusively the volume of trade, and secondly, not all outfitting agreements were signed before a notary. Because of these gaps in our information, the purpose of this chapter is not to write a history of whaling. We can simply look at this activity as part of a specific social and economic context, i.e., the Basque region, particularly the South, in the second half of the 16th century.

In a document written by the merchants of Bayonne in 1684 about their city's trade, they describe the northern Basque country as being composed of arid sands and barren lands, where the inhabitants could not harvest enough to feed themselves two months of the year.[1] On the Spanish side, the situation was hardly better since the land consisted of mountains which were suitable only for logging or mining.[2] From the beginning, therefore, the Basques had to seek some other means of trading

1 Maxime Dégros, *op. cit.*, No. 48 (1944), p. 77.

2 Julio Caro Baroja, *Los Vascos* (Madrid: Istmo, 1971), p. 195. The southern Basque region nevertheless possessed better resources than the northern region. Agriculture was more prosperous, the mountains held ore deposits, and the harbours were more suitable for shipping.

if they were to ensure their survival.[3] For several centuries, they found it in fishing in general and the whale hunt in particular. The Bayonne merchants' account adds that the only way for the inhabitants of Bayonne and the surrounding countryside to survive was to turn to the sea at their doorstep.[4] Had this account been written a century earlier, it would have been equally pertinent. A 19th-century author aptly summarized the situation when he said that for a man to take a fish out of the sea was the same as to take out a coin of the realm.[5] In Pierre Chaunu's words, the Basque provinces had been, so to speak, thrown into the sea at a very early date.[6]

At the end of the 15th century and the beginning of the 16th, various discoveries, new techniques and a spirit of modernism fostered the advent of a relatively well developed "commercial capitalism" in most western countries. As the cities grew and attracted an increasing number of inhabitants, there was a concomitant demand for both industrial and agricultural products, hence the need for more active and better organized trading. Commercial shipping was the most important component of this activity. The opening of new transatlantic routes in turn led to an increase in shipping and also shifted maritime activities toward Atlantic ports, resulting in what Pierre Chaunu describes as a major transformation in the geographic framework.[7] The trade in fish, which was the basis on which most countries established their commercial fleets and their navies, at the time held pride of place on the list of commercial activities. It could be said that the exploitation of the Newfoundland banks was "big business" in the late 1500s and early 1600s.[8] Laurier Turgeon has shown that this particular sector triggered a spectacular growth that evolved with the course of the European economic conjuncture until the end of the 16th century. The road to Terranova was then far busier than the one to South America.[9] Inured to the dangers of the Bay of Biscay, Basque sailors rapidly mastered the navigation of the North At-

---

3 Maxime Dégros, *op. cit.,* No. 48 (1944), p. 77.

4 *Ibid.*

5 Nicolas de Soraluce y Zubizarreta, *Introducción, capitulo 1 y otras descripciones de la memoria acerca del origen y curso de las pescas y pesquerías de ballenas y de bacalaos asi que sobre el descrubrimiento de los bancos e Isla de Terranova* (Vitoria: Hijos de Mantele, 1878), p. 11.

6 Pierre Chaunu, "Les routes espagnoles de l'Atlantique," in *Travaux du Colloque international d'histoire maritime* (9th, Seville, 1967) [Paris: S.E.V.P.E.N., 1967], p. 107.

7 Pierre and Huguette Chaunu, *Séville et l'Atlantique: 1504-1650* (Paris: Armand Colin, 1955), Vol. 8, part 1, p. 5.

8 Pierre Chaunu, "Les routes...," *op. cit.,* p. 109.

9 Laurier Turgeon, "Pêcheurs basques...," *op.cit.,* p. 2.

lantic and the boreal seas, and quickly acquired a reputation as skilled, experienced mariners. Fortunate in having easy access to the ocean and convenient, fortified Spanish ports, they could draw in addition on abundant resources in timber, iron and hemp, the three main necessities for shipbuilding in the 16th century.

Shipbuilding

Notarized deeds of the southern Basque region in the years between 1550 and 1590 contain several dozen contracts relating to shipbuilding or to supplies of timber, nails or other materials. Obviously these contracts represent only a small part of the total number of ships built during that period. In his *Navegantes Guipuzcoanos*, published in Madrid in 1903, the historian Ramon Seoane y Ferrer lists 46 contracts for the province of Guipuzcoa alone,[10] even though by that time the largest archival collection, the San Sebastián archives, could no longer be included in the research, having been destroyed during the Napoleonic Wars. Michael Barkham estimates that the *annual* production of the southern Basque region in the second half of the 16th century amounted to 20 ships of 100 *toneladas* or more.[11]

The main shipyards were located in Bilbao, Zarauz, Deva, Zumaya, Guetaria, Usurbil, Orio, Irun, Renteria, Lezo, and of course, Pasajes. By the end of the 15th century these towns were already renowned for the soundness of their ships and their experienced mariners. The chronicler Hernando del Pulgar said of the inhabitants of the provinces of Biscaya and Guipuzcoa that they outshone all other nations in the art of navigation and were very courageous in naval combats.[12] In his *Suma de Geografía*, Fernandez de Enciso reported that many sturdy ships were being built in these two provinces and that these vessels outnumbered those in all of Spain.[13]

The Basque region did indeed have all the components required for an active shipbuilding industry: hemp came from the north, resin from the Landes in the south-

10 Ramon Seoane y Ferrer, *op. cit.*, p. 95.

11 Michael Barkham, "Sixteenth Century Spanish Basque Ships and Shipbuilding: the multipurpose nao," in *Postmedieval Boat and Ship Archaeology* (Stockholm: Swedish National Maritime Museum, 1985), p. 122.

12 Julio Caro Baroja, *op.cit.*, p. 71.

13 Ramon de Berraondo, "Apuntes retrospectivos de la ciudad de San Sebastián," *Vida Vasca,* No. 6 (1929), p. 135.

west of France, timber from the Pyrenees and the Bayonne area, and iron from the mountains of Biscaya province. The region also had an abundance of skilled workers who had formed corporations of carpenters, coopers, blacksmiths, caulkers, rope-makers, sailmakers, armorers and the like. According to Lope Martinez de Isasti, in 1626 the province of Guipuzcoa alone still had 80 large and 38 small forges, whose total annual production reached 120,000 quintals of iron, one quintal being equal to 150 pounds.[14] The iron was renowned throughout Europe for its quality, and a large amount of it was used in shipbuilding.

All kinds of ships were built in these yards: caravels, galleons, *felipotes, ourques, pataches,* galleys, galleasses, *zabras,* pinnaces and *naos.* These ships were used for fishing, of course, but also for trade, piracy and even war. When hostilities arose, the king would place an embargo on various vessels, use them to make up his fleet, and then return them to their owners and their former uses when peace reigned once more. This is why it is difficult to distinguish between commercial vessels and warships of that period — to a large extent the war fleet *was* the fishing fleet. It was only under Philip V that the Navy became an entity separate from the merchant marine.

In the 1570s, however, Basque shipbuilding began to wane. One of the reasons was the exhaustion of the timber reserves. Already in 1561, Sir Thomas Chamberlain was writing that the Basques had cut down the best trees without planting others, with the result that there was hardly any timber left for shipbuilding — hence the increase in prices, which had doubled in 30 years.[15] Also in short supply was the wood used in forge furnaces, where the smelting process for iron production required enormous quantities of fuel. It is clear that without policies fostering the renewal of their resources, the Basque provinces could not meet the demand, given the smallness of their territory.

Biscayans, for their part, attributed the crisis in shipbuilding to the king, who had often requisitioned their ships but had paid them so little that they had had to turn to other economic pursuits. This practice resulted in depleting the ports of both men and ships.

---

14 Francisco M. Labayen, "Ferrerías y ferrones," *Vida Vasca,* No. 30 (1953), p. 100.

15 H.A. Innis, *op.cit.,* p. 57.

As well, it appears that toward the end of the 16th century Basque shipbuilding practices lagged far behind those of northern countries. While in England ships were now lighter, more manoeuvrable and better equipped, Basque builders were hemmed in by traditionalism and conservatism and continued to build ponderous vessels that were not easily helmed. The defeat of the Armada emphasized the growing gap between the two techniques. Now obsolete, the Basque shipbuilding industry, which had once sustained thousands of inhabitants from among whom had sprung famous explorers, navigators, admirals and builders, was about to give way to more innovative competitors, thus sounding the knell for Basque whaling.

Outfitting the Ships

While for decades shipbuilding and its related industries provided a livelihood for a large segment of the Basque population, the business of outfitting the ships also played a role in strengthening the region's economy. At a time when Normans, Bretons and Rochelais were sailing vessels of 50 to 100 tons, the Basques had ships of 200 to 700 *toneladas* manned by crews of 40 to 100 men. Outfitting these ships called for considerable investment. Notarized deeds refer to numerous loans obtained by individuals, or more often by several persons, for the purpose of outfitting a ship. These loans could easily reach 800 ducats or 24 times the annual wage of a carpenter.[16] This money was then paid out to various ship chandlers for the purchase of victuals, whaling gear, ropes, casks, and so on. This meant profits for suppliers as well as the creation of hundreds of secondary jobs. It has been estimated that apart from the 4000 men who made up Basque whaling crews in 1571, there were an additional 20,000 people living off the sea.[17] Terranova was so to speak the "breadbasket" of the Basques.

This economic upswing was of short duration. At the end of the 16th century, capital came mainly from the large centres such as Bordeaux and La Rochelle where

16 In 1561, outfitting the *Madalena* alone cost 248 ducats. The full cost for the *Trinidad* was evaluated at 800 ducats and that for the *Santa Maria de Yciar* at 854 ducats. The Basque Country. AHPG. Oñate. Partido de Vergara, Vol. 2578, reg. 4, fol. 9v; reg. 7, fol. 3; reg. 12, fol. 23. The equipping of the *Santo Crucifijo de Burgos* in 1565 is stated to have cost 36,824 *reales*, or 3273 ducats - a very considerable amount. The Basque Country. AGDG. Tolosa. Corregimiento, Civiles Elorza, Legajo 213, fol. 100.

17 Laurier Turgeon, "Pêcheurs basques...," *op.cit.*, p. 18. Maxime Dégros, *op. cit.*, No. 40 (1942), p. 27.

people were more sophisticated about business matters and more likely to contemplate far-flung expeditions. As well, because their land was small the Basques were often forced to obtain their supplies elsewhere. Not only did outfitting costs increase as a result, but also the region was deprived of the considerable economic benefits associated with ship chandlery, and a large segment of the population that depended directly on the fisheries was forced to resettle in other lands.[18] Without their outlets, the outfitters could no longer manage to cover their costs, and gradually they abandoned the whale fishery that had so long been one of the Basque area's economic strengths.

Distribution of Income from the Hunt

In the days when it was still profitable, whale hunting did entail sizable investment but it also promised very substantial profits. A 17th-century account stated that when it was successful, whaling was "the noblest and most lucrative of all types of fishing."[19]

Toward the middle of the 16th century, a ship with a full cargo might bring back 1000 to 1500 barrels of oil, depending on its capacity.[20] At an average price of six ducats a barrel, the oil cargo alone could easily be worth 6000 to 9000 ducats.[21] In addition, there was the whalebone harvest, which from the 1580s on was worth at least as much as the oil.[22] In a single season, a ship could therefore easily bring back

---

18 In the 18th century, the Basques had to import more than half of their victuals. Laurier Turgeon, "Pêches basques...," *op.cit.*, p. 239.

19 Maxime Dégros, *op.cit.*, No. 44 (1943), p. 99.

20 The Greenland whale could produce 40 to 90 barrels of oil; a full cargo therefore required the capture of 20 whales per ship.

21 Transposing prices from one era to another is always somewhat risky. Nevertheless it is of interest to try to estimate the value of a barrel of whale oil in modern terms. The calculation is based on two items that are well documented, the price of a barrel of oil, which in the 1560s was six ducats (it was to rise to eight ducats after 1570), and the wages of a ship's carpenter, which amounted to 35 ducats. Using a conservative ratio of 1:5 for these two items and taking as our reference point an annual salary of $25,000 paid to a modern carpenter, a barrel of whale oil would be worth $5000 today. A cargo of 1000 barrels would therefore be worth the tidy sum of five million dollars.

22 In 1596, Captain Domingo de Aizarna had 4500 baleen plates loaded onto the *Catalina*; according to various witnesses, the value of this cargo was at least equal to the 250 barrels of oil that the ship could have taken on instead. The Basque Country. ADGD. Tolosa. Corregimiento, Civiles Lecuona, Legajo 9, file 203, fol. 1r.

a cargo valued at 10,000 ducats, which would amply cover the cost of building and outfitting a new galleon and leave a substantial profit besides.[23] Not all ships came back with a full cargo though.

Several documents, including the statement settling the accounts for the cargo of the *San Nicolas* in 1566, show that in the southern part of the Basque lands the product of the hunt was divided into three parts; the crew received one-third, the owner one-fourth, and the outfitters the rest.[24] One-third of the barrels attributed to the shallop crews (10) and one-third of those of the flensers (2) were added to the outfitters' portion, in compensation for the equipment they were required to provide for these men. In the case of the *San Nicolas*, which carried 1195 barrels, the outfitters' portion was therefore increased to 509½ barrels. On the other hand they had to pay various bonuses to the whalemen, for reasons that are not specified. These bonuses amounted to 113 barrels, thus leaving only 396½ for the outfitters to cover their costs and show a profit. At a unit price of six ducats a barrel in the 1560s, their portion thus came to about 2400 ducats. From this amount they had to deduct the advances they had received before the voyage for equipping the ship, and pay the interest. The interest was collected in shares and the amount could vary from one-tenth of a share to two shares depending on the amount of the loan. In general, the lender demanded one share for every 60 ducats that he advanced to the outfitters;[25] one share being worth 20 ducats, the rate of interest was therefore 33 percent.[26] It should be explained that the figure of 20 ducats was arrived at using statements for two loans contracted one day apart by the same borrower. According to the first document, the debtor was to remit the capital of 30 ducats plus one half-share in interest; in the second document, he was to pay 30 ducats plus 10 ducats — therefore one share must have equalled 20 ducats. The rate of interest mentioned above was confirmed in a few other documents, including an acknowledgement of debt signed by Juanes de Ibaneta for a voyage to Terranova in 1583, and the account books of two wealthy lenders of

23 According to various notarized deeds, the construction of a 300-*tonelada* galleon cost about 1700 ducats, and outfitting it about 800, for a total of 2500 ducats. The Basque Country. AHPG. Oñate. Partido de Vergara. The Basque Country. AGDG. Tolosa. Corregimiento, Ejecutivos Elorza, Legajo 229, fol. 3v.

24 Mariano Ciriquiain Gaiztarro, *Los Vascos..., op. cit.*, p. 258. The Basque Country. AGDG. Tolosa. Corregimiento, Civiles Lecuona, Legajo 9, file 203; Ejecutivos Elorza, Legajo 229.

25 The Basque Country. AHPG. Oñate. Partido de Vergara, vol. 2579, reg. 4, fol. 31.

26 *Ibid.*, Vol. 2579, reg. 8, fol. 73. Another document, however, dated 1582, mentions an interest of 26 ducats on an investment of 260 ducats or 10 percent. *Ibid.*, Vol. 2578, reg. 12, fol. 18.

San Sebastián, Domingo de Hoa and Dona Mariana de Rober y Salinas. According to these books, promissory notes were granted at rates ranging between 26 and 30 percent.[27] Outfitters could repay the capital and interest in money or in kind within 10 to 45 days of the ship's return. They could then realize the remainder in cash.

The shipowner's portion, one-fourth of the cargo or 298½ barrels in the case of the *San Nicolas*, was also reduced by bonuses paid to the *oficiales* on board, among them the captain, boatswain, carpenter, caulker and gunner. These bonuses amounted to 26½ barrels, leaving a net income of 272 barrels for the owner, although the latter may have been required to pay out certain additional dues. A trial held in San Sebastián in 1561 mentions dues of two percent of the proceeds of the Terranova hunt to be paid by shipowners to their parish. In 1564, the proceedings of the municipal council of Motrico also mention dues of one percent to be paid to the church of Notre-Dame by ships returning from American waters.[28]

The third and last portion of the cargo was paid to the crew. For the *San Nicolas* in 1566 this amounted to one-third of the cargo or 399 barrels.[29] However, the document does not state precisely how much was received by each member of the crew. The distribution would have been based on each man's duty aboard the ship and was undoubtedly unequal. Thus the captain might receive up to 30 barrels, whereas a simple seaman would have to be content with four to six barrels, and an apprentice two or three. A document dated 1565 specifies that a harpooner generally received three shares or *soldadas*: one for his person, one for his work and one for the boat he was required to provide. Each share being worth 20 ducats, a harpooner would therefore earn a minimum per season of 10 barrels of oil, worth six ducats each in the 1560s.[30] In 1581, the harpooner Juan Perez de Larrea had entered into an agreement with the outfitters of the *Catalina* that was to earn him 30 barrels of oil for himself and his son if the hold was full.[31] Of course if the season was a poor one and the ship

27 The Basque Country. AGDG. Tolosa. Corregimiento, Ejecutivos Uria, Legajo 2, fol. 60, and René Bélanger, *op.cit.*, p. 71. However, the value of a share — and therefore the interest rate — may have varied as a function of the total proceeds of the cargo.

28 The Basque Country. AHPG. Oñate. Partido de Vergara, Vol. 2579, reg. 5, fol. 8.

29 This distribution is confirmed by several documents, including a trial in 1596. The Basque Country. AGDG. Tolosa. Corregimiento, Civiles Lecuona, Legajo 9, file 203, fol. 17r.

30 The Basque Country. AGDG. Tolosa. Corregimiento, Civiles Elorza, Legajo 65, fol. 9v. The same information appears in a 1571 trial. The Basque Country. AHPG. Oñate. Pleitos civiles, Perez Alonzo fenecidos, box 455-1.

31 The Basque Country. AGDG. Tolosa. Corregimiento, Ejecutivos Elorza, Legajo 229, fol. 1r.

returned with its hold only partially filled, each person's portion would be reduced accordingly. As it happened, the ship brought back only 460 of the 780 barrels it could hold, and Larrea and his son received only 17 barrels instead of 30.[32] No doubt this was the reason that many mariners hired themselves out for fixed wages rather than percentages. This method of hiring, mentioned by a witness in a trial in 1570, ensured that they would receive the amount determined before departure, whether or not the ship returned full.[33]

It appears that, failing a specific agreement, the crew was not entitled to a portion of the whalebone, or so we may deduce from a suit brought by Juanes de Labao against Captain Domingo de Aizarna in 1596.[34] The latter had loaded the *Catalina de San Vicente* with 4500 baleen plates, using the space normally occupied by 250 barrels of oil and thus reducing the whalemen's portion accordingly. On behalf of the crew, Labao claimed as compensation one-third of the value of the whalebone, but the captain refused to pay, arguing that this valuable cargo had always belonged exclusively to the outfitters. It should be mentioned that before the 1580s, whalebone fetched such a low price that it was usually left in Terranova; no one was interested in claiming a share of this commodity.

Whalemen were paid from the day they were hired and were required to help load the ship.[35] No doubt they received an advance before departure, since in 1613 the king ordered that one-fifth of this allowance be withheld until the day of sailing.[36] These advances, which ranged between 12 and 25 percent, would be used to purchase their wearing apparel for the voyage and to support their families while they were away. Once all the deductions had been made, the crew's portion, which in principle was 33 percent, often amounted to less than 10 percent of the cargo's value.[37]

In the northern Basque country in the 16th century, costs and proceeds were most often divided into three equal portions: one to the owner for having provided the ship; one to the outfitters for supplying the victuals and the equipment; and the third to the crew for their labour. Each party then subdivided its portion in accordance

32 *Ibid.*

33 The Basque Country. AGDG. Tolosa. Corregimiento, Civiles Elorza, Legajo 172, fol. 36r.

34 The Basque Country. AGDG. Tolosa. Corregimiento, Civiles Lecuona, Legajo 9, file 203, fol. 10r.

35 The Basque Country. AGDG. Tolosa. Corregimiento, Civiles Elorza, Legajo 65, fol. 28v.

36 Spain. Madrid. Museo Naval. Vargas Ponce Collection, Vol. III, fol. 81.

37 Laurier Turgeon, "Pêches basques...," *op.cit.*, p. 332.

with individual responsibilities or investments. In wartime, this tripartite division could be amended in the outfitters' favour to the detriment of the owner and the crew. This practice became generalized toward the end of the 16th century, a period shadowed by the Wars of Religion.[38]

In general, even though whale hunting was less profitable for simple mariners than for the owners or outfitters, it still provided them with a fair income. An oarsman could earn in a single season the equivalent of four to six barrels of oil; in the 1560s this was about 25 to 35 ducats. At that time, skilled workers such as carpenters earned about 35 ducats over a whole year.[39] As well, seamen were fed and housed and had four months free in which to augment their income. According to some documents, however, it would seem that these few months of rest were often devoted to carousing and revelry that rapidly depleted the funds accumulated during the eight months of work.[40] When the time came to depart for a new season, the reprobates had to borrow once more to purchase their wearing apparel and to have something left over for a few treats during the voyage. Although such accounts are numerous, it is not unlikely that there were just as many sailors who did not squander their wages in degenerate pursuits. Discretion being the better part of virtue, however, such men are less likely to be mentioned in the contemporary documentation.

Insurance

Aiming to minimize their losses as much as possible when either ship or cargo was damaged, or to underwrite a loan, both shipowners and outfitters took out insurance to cover possible mishaps. The number of whalemen in the southern Basque country who did so is not known.[41] However, in this area as in many others, the

38 Laurier Turgeon, "Les pêches françaises...," *op.cit.*, p. 21.

39 With 10 ducats, a man could buy 575 pounds of dried cod or 250 litres of whale oil or 5 hogsheads of cider or 300 pounds of bacon. These data were taken from a compilation based on several notarized documents in southern Basque archives.

40 A 17th-century account refers to "those who spend the night in debauchery after supping in public houses and who make insolences, gathering together, running through the streets with weapons, firing pistol shots, rattling their sabres, banging on doors and other illicit acts, disturbing and alarming upright citizens at rest. And not content with this, going about in groups and bringing together persons who might in devotion have gone to hear divine service, and performing dances before said divine service either publicly in the streets or in private homes, even in public houses and billiard rooms showing great contempt for God and human faith." René Bélanger, *op.cit.*, p. 32.

Basques were ahead of other European countries. When the first insurance contracts appeared in England in about 1604, Basques had already benefited from this type of protection for over fifty years.[42] Insurance was taken out in Burgos, or, more usually, through an agent residing in the Basque region. It applied either to the hull, artillery and munition, or to the cargo. It could be valid for the outbound voyage, the season in Terranova and the return, or for season and return only. Between 1565 and 1573, the average rate for protection throughout the voyage was 15 percent on the hull and 14 percent on the cargo; for protection one-way only, the rates were 10 percent and 9 percent respectively. These rates were among the highest charged by Burgos underwriters, indicating that whale hunting in Terranova was still a relatively perilous undertaking, mainly because of the pirates and privateers who awaited the ships' return. The criteria for determining the rates were based on the itinerary chosen, the goods carried, the period of the year during which the voyage took place, the ship and the name of the master, whether the vessel was sailing singly or as part of a fleet, the flag under which it was sailing, and the presence of pirates or privateers on the high seas. Southern Basque ships received less favorable rates than did northern ones because they had a reputation for being less safe.[43]

At the beginning of the 1570s, the average insured amounts were 901 ducats for the cargo and 1454 for the hull. Contracts were usually signed in mid-June for expeditions insured for the entire voyage, and in mid-October for those protected one-way only. Commercial fairs were held twice a year at Medina del Campo, and the premiums were paid at the next fair following the signature of the contract. The insured party often signed several contracts for various amounts for the same expedition, but the total amount of the contracts could not exceed 90 percent of the insurable value.[44] Archival documentation mentions the case of a whaling ship

---

41 The earliest insurance contract for Terranova that has come to light is dated 1547. Selma Barkham, "Burgos Insurance for Basque Ships: Maritime Policies from Spain, 1547-1592," *Archivaria,* No. 11 (Winter 1980-81), p. 92.

42 In the beginning it was the practice for the insurer not only to cover the risks of the voyage but also to advance the amount insured, i.e., the agreed-upon value of the ship or of the cargo. This practice continued for many years. The amount was actually paid before departure by the insurer and was reimbursed only if the vessel returned safely to port. Jacques Heers, "Rivalité ou collaboration de la terre et de l'eau," in *Travaux du Colloque international d'histoire maritime* (7th, Vienna, 1965) [Paris: S.E.V.P.E.N., 1965], p. 37.

43 Manuel Basas Fernandez, *El seguro maritimo en Burgos; siglo XVI* (Bilbao: Estudios de Deusto, 1963), p. 110.

44 *Ibid.,* p. 91.

owner who had insured his vessel in various places for a total amount far in excess of its value. After the ship burned in the Pasajes harbour in 1572, the insurers refused to pay, claiming that one could not take out two policies on a single vessel.[45]

Markets for Whale Products

From the 15th to the 18th century, utilization of both whale oil and whalebone remained essentially the same, but the range of available markets broadened considerably with the continually increasing demand. Both northern and southern Basques had foreign as well as domestic outlets. In the French domestic market, wholesalers purchased goods from the outfitters and marketed them through the distribution networks they controlled. Resales were parcelled out and reparcelled out among endless layers of middlemen. The oil came in at Bayonne and at Saint-Jean-de-Luz. In the 17th century, 500 large barrels fulfilled the needs of the Labourd region.[46] The rest was forwarded mainly to the textile and soap factories of the Languedoc and to the province of Béarn and the Gascony region. In Spain, the oil came in at Bilbao for routing to Castile and the valley of the Ebro and to San Sebastián for export to Navarra for use mainly in lighting, in the manufacture of broadcloth and in tanning. In 1576, one apothecary alone purchased eighteen 400-pound barrels of whale oil.[47]

The foreign market was much more complex. Basque whalemen usually sailed directly to Terranova, but upon their return they might unload cargo at Le Havre, Nantes, or Bristol or other ports on the North Atlantic or the Channel. These major centres had the enormous advantage of being located close to the most important consumers' markets in northern Europe. For these cities whale oil was an alternative to Mediterranean vegetable oils. After delivering their cargoes, some Basque whalemen would load their ships with goods that were unavailable in their own country, such as salt and grain.[48]

45 The Basque Country. AGDG. Tolosa. Corregimiento, Ejecutivos Uria, Legajo 1, fol. 24

46 Maxime Dégros, *op.cit.*, No. 44 (1943), p. 103.

47 The Basque Country. AHPG. Oñate. Partido de Vergara, Vol. 2580, reg. 3, fol. 55.

48 Iñaki Zumalde, *op.cit.*, February 24, 1980, p. 4.

However, most whalers preferred to return directly to their home ports and export their products from there. According to an account dated 1775, northern Basques used to export half, and sometimes as much as two-thirds, of their oil to Spain.[49] Bilbao, the capital of Biscaya, and San Sebastián, the town with the most active economy in Guipuzcoa, were the two largest oil export centres in the region. Agents of foreign merchants were stationed there on a permanent basis for the purpose of making their oil purchases. At the time, oil was second only to iron on the list of Basque exports. Over the winter of 1565-66, two merchants, Geronimo de Salamanca Santa Cruz and Antonio de Salazar, between them exported 28,000 ducats' worth of oil to northern Europe.[50] In the same year, Bordeaux merchants were also sending barrels of whale oil to Middelburg in Zellande."[51] This era might be called the golden age of whaling.

Beginning in the 1570s, however, Basque whaling in Labrador began a rapid and irremediable decline. The two merchants with exports worth 28,000 ducats in 1565 were down to only 2200 ducats twenty years later.[52] Also in 1585, an order from the Junta of Guipuzcoa forbade the mariners of that province to sail on French ships for fear that they would impart their technical knowledge to foreigners.[53] This kind of government intervention may indicate that it was becoming increasingly difficult to outfit local ships and that whalemen had no alternative but to hire themselves out to competitors, as they did a few decades later in Spitsbergen. Already much on the wane, Basque whaling lost still more ground after the defeat of the Armada and the signing of the treaty of 1604 which enabled the British to export their fish to Spain. By 1620 the southern Basques ceased going to Labrador altogether.

With the southern Basques out of the picture, the northern Basques had a monopoly on whaling, and the centre of activity shifted westward into the Gulf of St. Lawrence and the St. Lawrence River itself. Champlain, visiting Tadoussac in June 1626, met some Basques who had come to hunt whales around Sept-îles.[54] However,

49 René Bélanger, *op.cit.*, p. 27.

50 Selma Barkham, "Burgos...," *op.cit.*, p. 98. According to an insurance document dated 1565, oil intended for exportation was worth about eight ducats a barrel. Manuel Basas Fernandez, *op.cit.*, p. 63.

51 France. Bordeaux. ADG. Notaire Brigot, 3E2418, fol. 76.

52 Selma Barkham, "Burgos...," *op.cit.*, p. 98.

53 Henry Harrisse, *op.cit.*, p. 61.

54 Marcel Moussette, "La pêche de la baleine; méthodes de capture de la baleine utilisées dans le golfe et l'estuaire du Saint-Laurent," *Revue d'histoire de la Gaspésie*, Vol. 10, No. 1 (Jan.-Mar. 1972), p. 19.

northern Basques too began to encounter difficulties with the hunt. In 1550 the whale hunt accounted for almost 66 percent of the Bordeaux trade; by 1585 it was down to 33 percent.[55] Although in decline, the industry did survive until the 18th century, when it eventually died out.

***

The reasons that led the Basques to abandon the whale hunt along the coasts of North America are many and diverse. Some authors believe that the change came as a direct outcome of the discovery of new grounds in Spitsbergen at the beginning of the 17th century. Others associate the decline with the numerous wars fought by European powers at the end of the 16th century, of which the Basques were often victims. Other reasons cited by historians to explain the Basques' departure from Labrador are the lag in the development of Basque shipbuilding technology, their increasingly unfriendly relations with the indigenous peoples, a growing preference for trading in furs rather than fish or whale products, a noticeable decrease in whale stocks, the adverse policies adopted by metropolitan governments, and the defeat of the Armada.[56]

The primary reason for the Basques' departure, however, lies in an unfavorable combination of circumstances arising out of the major social and economic changes that occurred in Europe at the time. The end of the 16th century was indeed a very dismal period for the European economy in general and for wage workers in particular. As a result of massive arrivals of precious metals in Europe, prices were tripling, while wages barely rose. Whaling suffered the consequences of the crisis. The barrel of oil that was worth 6 ducats in the 1560s was selling for 12 and even 15 ducats thirty years later.[57] Other factors played a role as well: numerous wars which ruined a good part of the Basque fleet; poor harvests which forced the fishermen to forego voyages that took them away from home for several months, so that they could look after the more pressing needs of their families; increases in grain prices and in ship chandlery costs; the shrinking of the Basque shipbuilding industry; and lastly the exodus of whalemen who sought their fortune elsewhere. Discouraged by numerous

55 Laurier Turgeon, "Les pêches françaises...," *op.cit.,* p. 10.

56 Jean-Pierre Proulx, *op.cit.,* p. 24.

57 The Basque Country. AGDG. Tolosa. Corregimiento, Ejecutivos Elorza, Legajo 345, fol. 37v.

failures, outfitters were no longer willing to bank their capital on such a risky undertaking. These obstacles affecting the whaling industry in turn led to slowdowns in the secondary industries and to underemployment, itself followed by a massive emigration of the labour force. By 1602, there were only seven whaling ships in Terranova. Various attempts on the part of national rulers to redress the situation might have succeeded were it not for the Dutch. After learning whaling techniques from the Basques, the students rapidly outshone the masters, because their political and economic organization was better structured, more effective and more powerful. In order to contend with Dutch competition, the Basques would have had to increase their tonnage so as to increase production and thus maintain prices at low levels, but they no longer had the capacity to do this. With a declining population, the Basque region was short of skilled labour in both the whaling and the shipbuilding sectors. Ships were even being purchased from Dutch competitors. Nor could the Basques hope to rival their competitors' prices, because their hinterland's resources were too limited to supply a fleet comparable to that of Holland. They were forced to import basic staples and as a result the costs of outfitting their whaling expeditions rose still higher, and they simply could not remain competitive. Customs restrictions notwithstanding, Dutch oil continued to infiltrate French ports at a price lower than the Basques', thus depriving them of their outlets. Had the Basques been able, like the people of Saint-Malo, to diversify their foreign trade by exchanging their whaling products for other wares instead of currency, their industry would no doubt have better withstood their competitors' inroads. In short, in order to compete with Dutch whaling, Basque whaling would have had to reach a level of development that was precluded by the region's deficiency in both material and human resources. Therein lies the main reason for the waning of this industry in the 16th century.

Conclusion

In his work on Christopher Columbus, the historian Jacques Heers ponders the reasons that led men to become whalers.[1] Clearly, a search for plausible answers would require research on the ships' crews, a social and economic analysis of the seafarers' milieu, and a study of their social and geographic origins and the methods of recruitment. All these studies are still to be made. However, from the research so far conducted on the history of Basque whaling, we now know that this industry presupposed a strong organization, a hierarchy, and uncommon discipline. As well, it required local buying power high enough to afford a product as expensive as oil, agriculture prosperous enough to support the provisioning of expeditions, an abundant workforce available for six to eight months of the year, and an expertise and industrial infrastructure developed enough to take on shipbuilding and navigation. For 600 years, the Basque region possessed all of these material and human assets which ensured the profitability of the undertaking.

This exploit is all the more remarkable in that it was the work of a people inhabiting a very small area with relatively limited resources. It was largely the whale fishery that gave the Basques their spirit of adventure and their reputation as expert mariners in an era when the sea was still a terrifying world for most people, as can be glimpsed in the proverbs circulating at that time.[2] As far as the 19th-century French

---

1 Jacques Heers, "Christophe Colomb...", *op.cit.*, p. 59.

2 The Romans said: "Praise the sea, but stay on the shore." A Russian saying similarly advised: "Praise the sea - while sitting on the stove." [Warm tiled stoves were traditionally used as beds in olden-days Russia.] A character in Erasmus's *Naufragium* opines that it is foolish to trust in the sea. Even among the seafaring Dutch there was a saying that it was better to be on a barren heath in an old cart than out at sea in a new ship. Jean Delumeau, *La peur en Occident: XIVe-XVIIIe siècles* (Paris: Fayard, 1978), p. 31.

historian Jules Michelet was concerned, it was through the whale hunt that the world was discovered.[3] The Basques may indeed have been the nation that made the single greatest contribution to this discovery, both through their own voyages and through the course they charted for those who came in their wake.

The traces of the Basque whalers' lives found in present-day Red Bay have made it a place of national historic importance to Canada. The site has now attained international renown, both historically and archaeologically. We had long suspected that Basque whalers were hunting in our waters in the 16th century, but before the commencement of this vast research project, there was no basis to gauge the economic and social impact of their presence here. We now know that Red Bay was the focal point of a major economic activity at a period in Canadian history that until recently was little known. The research accomplished in the last few years now compels Canadian historians to rewrite the history of the last half of the 16th century, and has revealed heretofore unknown information concerning whaling techniques and shipbuilding. We are now able to reconstitute most of the components of a 17th-century merchant vessel. This is a precedent in the history of shipbuilding and it fills a considerable gap in our knowledge. Before the discovery of the wreck in Red Bay, historians knew more about the ships of the Roman and medieval navies than about those which sailed the Terranova runs four hundred years ago.

These new data could also open doors to subjects of historical research that are as yet unexplored. For example, it would be interesting to determine whether the Basque whaling monopoly in the 16th century might not have hampered colonial settlement in New France. The entrepreneurs who had a stake in the highly lucrative whale oil trade looked askance at the settlement on American soil of pioneers protected by their metropolitan government, because the new residents represented a threat to their monopoly. Knowing the economic impact of this activity in the 16th century, we would not be surprised to learn that the various governments of the period acquiesced in the demands of the oil and cod producers and suppliers. We might also study the process of acculturation that may have resulted from the contacts between indigenous peoples and Europeans, both in America and in Europe. The interest aroused by the Red Bay project should renew the impetus of research in other countries such as England, France, Spain and The Netherlands. Further studies will undoubtedly shed more light on this era, the first century of our modern history.

---

3 A. Thomazi, *Histoire de la pêche des âges de pierre à nos jours* (Paris: Payot, 1947), p. 363.

Bibliography

Agud, Manuel

Elementos de cultura material en el país vasco. Euskal Historia, San Sebastián, 1980.

Alden, Daurel

"Yankee Sperm Whalers in Brazilian waters, and the Decline of the Portuguese Whale-fishery, 1773-1801," *The Americas: A Quarterly Review of Inter-American Culture History*, Vol. 20, No. 3 (Jan. 1964), pp. 267-88.

Allen, J.A.

"The North Atlantic Right Whale and Its Near Allies," *Bulletin of the American Museum of Natural History*, Vol. 24 (1908), pp. 277-329.

Aramburu, J. de

Terranova: la ruta del bacalao. Caja de ahorros provincial, San Sebastián, 1972.

Areitio, Dario de

"La pesca de la ballena: notas de un pleito de principios del siglo XVII," *Revue internationale des études basques*, Vol. 17, No. 2 (1926), pp. 194-200.

Arne, P.

"La baleine des Basques," *Bulletin du Musée basque*, Vols. 18 and 19, Nos. 21-22 (1942-43), pp. 189-96.

Arnold, J. Barto

The Nautical Archaeology of Padre Island; the Spanish Shipwrecks of 1554. Academic Press, New York, 1978.

Arocena, Fausto

"Sintesis de la historia interna de Guipuzcoa," *Euskalerriaren Alde*, Vol. 19, Nos. 301 and 302 (n.d.), pp. 282-303.

Arque, P.

Géographie des Pyrénées françaises. No publisher, Paris, 1943.

Arriategui, Fabian de

"Los astilleros de San Sebastián," *Vida Vasca*, No. 39 (1962), p. 111.

Arrinda, A.

Euskalerria eta arrantza. Aurrezki Kutxa, Donostia, 1977.

Arteche, José de

"La oración de los balleneros," *Vida Vasca*, No. 30 (1953), pp. 116-17.

Audy, Michel, et al.

"Summary of Field Research Conducted in 1980 at Red Bay, Labrador, on the Underwater Remains of the *San Juan* and of thet Basque Whaling Station," *Research Bulletin*, No. 163 (July 1981), Parks Canada, Ottawa.

Ayerbe, Enrique, (ed.)

Itsasoa 3: Los Vascos en el marco atlantico norte. Siglos XVI y XVII. ETOR, San Sebastián, 1988.

Bailac, J.B.

Nouvelle chronique de la ville de Bayonne. Duhart-Fauvet, Bayonne, 1827.

Balasque, Jules

Études historiques de la ville de Bayonne. E. Laserre, Bayonne, 1869.

Ballesteros-Beretta, A.
La marina cantabra. Aldus Velarde, Santander, 1968.

Barbour, Violet
"Marine Risks and Insurance in the Seventeenth Century," *Journal of Economic and Business History*, Vol. 1 (1928-29), p. 561-96.

Bare, Gil
"Las antiguas industrias marítimas guipuzcoanas," *Vida Vasca*, Vol. 22 (1945), p. 113.

Barkham, Michael
Aspects of Life aboard Spanish Basque Ships during the 16th century with Special Reference to Terranova Whaling Voyages. Microfiche Report Series No. 75, Parks Canada, Ottawa, 1981.

——. "Report on 16th century Spanish Basque Shipbuilding ca. 1550-ca. 1600," Manuscript Report Series No. 422, Parks Canada, Ottawa, 1981.

——. "Sixteenth Century Spanish Basque Ships and Shipbuilding: the multipurpose nao," *Postmedieval Boat and Ship Archaeology*, Swedish National Maritime Museum, Stockholm, Report No. 20 (1985), pp. 113-35.

Barkham, Selma
"Building Materials for Canada, in 1556," *Bulletin of the Association for Preservation Technology*, Vol. 5, No. 4 (1973), pp. 93-94.

——. "Burgos Insurance for Basque ships: Maritime Policies from Spain, 1547-1592," *Archivaria*, No. 11 (Winter 1980-81), pp. 87-99.

——. "Documentary Evidence for 16th-century Basque Whaling Ships in the Strait of Belle Isle," in *Early European Settlement and Exploitation in Atlantic Canada*. Memorial University of Newfoundland, St. John's, Nfld., 1982, pp. 53-89.

——. "Finding Sources of Canadian History in Spain," *Canadian Geographic*, Vol. 100, No. 3 (June-July 1980), pp. 66-73.

——. "The Basques: Filling a Gap in our History between Jacques Cartier and Champlain," *Canadian Geographic*, Vol. 96, No. 1 (Feb-Mar 1978), pp. 8-19.

——. "The Identification of Labrador Ports in Spanish 16th century Documents," *The Canadian Cartographer*, Vol. 14, No. 1 (June 1977), pp. 1-9.

——. "First Will and Testament on the Labrador Coast," *The Geographical Magazine*, Vol. 49, No. 9 (June 1977), pp. 574-81.

Barkham, Selma, and Robert Grenier
"Divers Find Sunken Basque Galleon in Labrador," *Canadian Geographic*, Vol. 97, No. 3 (Dec. 1978-Jan. 1979), pp. 60-63.

Basas Fernandez, Manuel
El consulado de Burgos en el siglo XVI. Consejo superior de investigaciones cientificas; Escuela de historia moderna, Madrid, 1963.

——. *El seguro maritimo en Burgos; siglo XVI.* Estudios de Deusto, Bilbao, 1963.

Beaudoin, François
"Les bateaux de l'Adour," *Bulletin du Musée basque*, No. 48-49 (1970), pp. 49-144.

Bélanger, René
Les Basques dans l'estuaire du Saint-Laurent, 1535-1635. Montréal, Presses de l'Université du Québec, 1971.

Bellet, Adolphe
La grande pêche de la morue à Terre-Neuve depuis la découverte du Nouveau-Monde par les Basques au XIVe siècle. Augustin Challamel, Paris, 1902.

Berdeco, M.
"Coutumes morales du pays basque," in *La tradition au pays basque*. Elkar, Donostia, 1982.

Bernard, Jacques
"Les constructions navales à Bordeaux d'après les archives notariales du XVIe siècle," in *Travaux du Colloque international d'histoire maritime* (1st, Paris, 1956). S.E.V.P.E.N., Paris, 1957, pp. 31-52.

——. “Les types de navires ibériques et leur influence sur la construction navale dans les ports du sud-ouest de la France...,” in *Travaux du Colloque international d’histoire maritime* (5th, Lisbon, 1960). S.E.V.P.E.N., Lisbon, 1960, pp. 195-220.

——. *Navires et gens de mer de Bordeaux, 1400-1550.* S.E.V.P.E.N., Paris, 1968, 3 vols.

Berraondo, Ramon de

“Apuntes retrospectivos de la ciudad de San Sebastián,” *Vida Vasca*, No. 6 (1929), pp. 131-43.

——. “Los pescadores ante la historia,” *Euskalerriaren Alde*, Vol. 11, No. 205, pp. 241-48.

——. “Sellos medioevales de tipo naval,” *Vida Vasca*, No. 11 (1934), pp. 51-53.

——. “Aspectos vasconicos,” *Vida Vasca*, No. 8 (1931), pp. 153-61.

——. “Los Vascos en los viajes de Colon,” *Vida Vasca*, No. 10 (1933), pp. 73-77.

Blond, Georges

La grande aventure des baleines. Amiot-Dumont, Paris, 1953.

Boissonnade, P.

“La marine de commerce et de pêche du Pays basque et du Labourd au temps de Colbert,” *Bulletin de la section de géographie*, Vol. 49 (1934), pp. 43-87.

Braudel, Fernand

Civilisation matérielle et capitalisme; XVe-XVIIIe siècles. Armand Colin, Paris, 1967.

——. *Le monde de Jacques Cartier: l’aventure au 16e siècle.* Libre Expression, Montréal, 1984.

Browne, J. Ross

Etchings of a Whaling Cruise with Notes of a Sojourn on the Island of Zanzibar to which is Appended a Brief History of the Whale Fishery, its Past and Present Condition. Harper & Brothers, New York, 1846.

Budker, Paul

Whales and Whaling. G.G. Harrap, London, 1958.

Burton, Robert

The Life and Death of Whales. A. Deutsch, London, 1973.

Calle Iturrino, E.

Hombres de mar de Vizcaya. Caja de ahorros de Vizcaya. Bilbao, 1968.

Camino y Orella, D. Joaquin Antonio del

Historia de San Sebastián. Valverde, San Sebastián, 1963.

Cano, Thome

Arte para fabricar, fortificar y aparear naos. Livis Estupinan, Seville, 1611.

Caro Baroja, Julio

Ensayos sobre la cultura popular espanóla. Dosbe, Madrid, 1979.

——. *Introducción a la historia social y económica del pueblo vasco.* Txertoa, San Sebastián, 1980.

——. *Los Vascos.* Istmo, Madrid, 1971.

——. "Un introducción a la historia del pueblo vasco," *Boletin de la real sociedad vascongada de los amigos del país,* Vol. 12 (1956), p. 345.

Casado Soto, Jose Luis

Cantabria vista por viajeros de los siglos XVI y XVII. Diputacion de Santander, Santander, 1980.

——. *Cantabria a traves de su historia: la crisis del siglo XVI.* Diputacion provincial, Santander, 1979.

——. *Los pescadores de la villa de Santander entre los siglos XVI y XVII.* No publisher, Santander, 1978.

Casariego, J.E.

Los Vascos en la empresas marítimas de España. Junta Cultural de Vizcaya, Bilbao, 1952.

Cell, Gillian T.

English Enterprise in Newfoundland, 1577-1660. Toronto University Press, Toronto, 1969.

Chatterton, E. Keble

Whalers and Whaling: The Story of the Whaling Ships up to the Present Day. J.B. Lippincott, Philadelphia, 1926.

Chaunu, Pierre

"La tonelada espagnole aux XVIe et XVIIe siècles," in *Travaux du Colloque international d'histoire maritime* (1st, Paris, 1956). S.E.V.P.E.N., Paris, 1957, pp. 71-84.

——. "Les routes espagnoles de l'Atlantique," in *Travaux du Colloque international d'histoire maritime* (9th, Seville, 1967). S.E.V.P.E.N., Paris, 1969, pp. 97-130.

Chaunu, Pierre and Huguette Chaunu

Séville et l'Atlantique: 1504-1650. Armand Colin, Paris, 1955, 8 vols.

Ciriquiain Gaiztarro, Mariano

"Las primeras representaciones gráficas de embarcaciones del litoral vasco," *Boletin de la real sociedad vascongada de los amigos del país,* Vol. 10 (1954), pp. 57-70.

——. *Los Vascos en la pesca de la ballena.* Ediciones Vascas, San Sebastián, 1961.

——. *La pesca en el mar vasco.* Editoria nacional, Madrid, 1952.

——. "La pinaza en el litoral vasco," in *Homenaje a D. Joaquin Mendizabal.* Museo de San Telmo, San Sebastián, 1956.

——. *Los puertos marítimos vascongados.* No publisher, San Sebastián, 1951.

Clark, Grahame

"Whales as an Economic Factor in Prehistoric Europe," *Antiquity*, Vol. 21, No. 82 (June 1947), pp. 84-104.

Clavería, Carlos

"Los Vascos en el mar," *Vida Vasca*, No. 37 (1960), pp. 81-83.

——. *Los Vascos en el mar.* Aramburu, Pamplona, 1965.

Clayton, Lawrence
"Ships and Empire: The Case of Spain," *The Mariner's Mirror*, Vol. 62, No. 3 (Aug. 1976), pp. 235-48.

Cleirac, Étienne
Us et Coutumes de la Mer. Jean Lucas, Rouen, 1671.

Cobb, D.
"Basques Ships and Men," *The Mariner's Mirror*, Vol. 64, No. 3 (1978), pp. 209-16.

Conway, W. Martin
Early Dutch and English Voyages to Spitsbergen in the 17th Century. Hakluyt Society, London, 2nd series, No. 11 (1902).
——. *No Man's Land: A History of Spitsbergen from its Discovery in 1596 to the Beginning of the Scientific Explorations of the Country*. Cambridge University Press, Cambridge, 1906.

Cortazar, N. de
"Testimonios lingüísticos vascos en Islandia y Terranova," *Vida Vasca*, No. 45 (1968), pp. 153-55.

Courteault, Paul
Pour l'histoire de Bordeaux et du Sud-Ouest. Auguste Picard, Paris, 1914.

Cuzacq, René
"La pêche à Saint-Jean-de-Luz," *Revue géographique des Pyrénées et du Sud-Ouest*, Vol. 4, No. 1 (Jan. 15 1938), pp. 287-96.
——. *Les Basques chasseurs de baleines*. Published by author, Bayonne, 1972.

Daranatz, J.B.
"Autour de Bayonne du XVe au XVIIIe siècle d'après les archives notariales bayonnaises," *Bulletin de la Société des Sciences, Lettres et Arts de Bayonne*, No. 9 (1932), pp. 58-87; No. 11 (1933), pp. 5-35; No. 12 (1933), pp. 257-85; No. 13 (1934), pp. 188-96; No. 15 (1935), pp. 88-106; No. 16 (1935), pp. 258-85; No. 17

(1936), pp. 58-69; No. 19 (1936), pp. 193-203; No. 22 (1937), pp. 145-63; No. 23 (1937), pp. 235-54; No. 25 (1938), pp. 34-40; No. 26 (1938), pp. 217-37.

——. "À qui la baleine?" *Gure Herria*, Vol. 2, No. 11 (1921), pp. 667-69.

Dardel, Éric

État des pêches maritimes sur les côtes occidentales de la France au début du XVIIIe siècle. D'après les procès-verbaux de visite de l'Inspecteur des Pêches Le Masson du Parc, 1723-1732. André Tournon, Paris, 1941.

Dégros, Maxime

"La grande pêche basque des origines à la fin du XVIIIe siècle," *Bulletin de la Société des Sciences, Lettres et Arts de Bayonne*, No. 35 (1940), pp. 148-79; No. 37 (1941), pp. 27-33; No. 38 (1941), n.p.; No. 39 (1941), pp. 156-63; No. 40 (1942), pp. 26-29; No. 41 (1942), pp. 74-78; No. 42 (1942), n.p.; No. 43 (1943), pp. 45-59; No. 44 (1943), pp. 95-108; No. 45 (1943), pp. 165-83; No. 46 (1943), pp. 221-26; No. 47 (1944), pp. 18-28; No. 48, (1944), pp. 75-82; No. 49 (1944), pp. 127-31; No. 50 (1945), pp. 34-43.

Delmas, Juan E.

Guia historico-desciptiva del viajero en el Senorio de Vizcaya. Juan E. Delmas, Bilbao, 1864.

Delumeau, Jean

La peur en Occident (XVIe-XVIIIe siècles). A. Fayard, Paris, 1978.

Denoix, L.

"Caractéristiques des navires de l'époque des grandes découvertes," in *Travaux du Colloque international d'histoire maritime* (5th, Lisbon, 1960). S.E.V.P.E.N., Paris, 1960, pp. 137-47.

——. "Le bâtiment de commerce et la navigation après les grandes découvertes," in *Travaux du Colloque international d'histoire maritime* (1st, Paris, 1956). S.E.V.P.E.N., Paris, 1957, pp. 17-30.

——. "Les problèmes de la navigation au début des grandes découvertes," in *Travaux du Colloque international d'histoire maritime* (5th, Lisbon, 1960). S.E.V.P.E.N., Paris, 1960, pp. 131-39.

Diccionario geográfico de España
Real Academia de la Historia, Madrid, 1802.

Diderot, Denis
Encyclopédie ou dictionnaire raisonné des sciences, des arts et des métiers. Briasson, Paris, 1751.

Diez de Salazar Fernandez, Luis Miguel
El diezmo viejo y seco o diezmo de la mar de Castilla: siglo XIII-XVI. Gaficas Eset, San Sebastián, 1983.

Ducéré, Édouard
Dictionnaire historique de Bayonne. 2nd. ed. Laffitte, Marseille, 1974.
——. *Les pêcheurs basques à Terre-Neuve.* No publisher, place or date.
——. "Recherches historiques sur les corsaires de Saint-Jean-de-Luz," in *La tradition au Pays Basque.* Elkar, Donostia, 1982.

Duhamel du Monceau
Traité général des pêches et histoire des poissons qu'elles fournissent tant pour la subsistance des hommes que pour plusieurs autres usages qui ont rapport aux arts et au commerce. Desaint, Paris, 1782.

Dulles, Foster Rhea
Lowered Boats: A Chronicle of American Whaling. Harcourt, New York, 1933.

Duval, Jules
"Les pêches de Terre-Neuve," *Revue des Deux-Mondes*, Vol. 22 (1859), pp. 831-63.

Echaniz, N.
"Motrico, su vida y su historia," *Vida Vasca*, No. 45 (1968), pp. 113-15.

Echegaray, Bonifacio de

'La vida civil y mercantil de los Vascos," *Revue internationale des études basques*, Vols. 13 and 19 (1922-23).

Echegaray, Rafael Gonzalez

Balleneros Cantabros. Institucion cultural de Cantabria, Santander, 1978.

Enciclopedia general ilustrada del país vasco

Aunamendi, San Sebastián, 1970- .

Escagües y Javierre, Idisoro

"Los astilleros vizcainos," *Vida Vasca*, Vol. 61 (1964), pp. 201.

——. "La economia del mar en Vizcaya," *Vida Vasca*, Vol. 32 (1955), pp. 190-97.

Fabié, Antonio Maria

Estudio sobre la organización y costumbres del País Vascongado. Fortanet, Madrid, 1896.

Faucher de Saint-Maurice, M.

Le Canada et les Basques. A. Côté, Québec, 1879.

Fauteux, J.N.

Essai sur l'industrie au Canada sous le régime français. Proulx, Québec, 1927.

——. "Privilège exclusif pour la pêche de la baleine," *Bulletin des recherches historiques*, Vol. 52, No. 3 (Mar. 1946), pp. 78-79.

Feduchi, Luis

Arquitectura popular espanola. No pubisher, Barcelona, 1979.

Fernandez Duro, Cesareo

Disquisiciones nauticas. Impresor de Camara de S.M., Madrid, 1876-81, 6 vols.

——. "El descubrimiento de Terranova," *Euskal Erria*, Vol. 15, No. 226 (1886), pp. 325-27.

Fournier, George

Hydrographie contenant la théorie et la pratique de toutes les parties de la navigation. Jean Dupuis, Paris, 1667.

France

Bordeaux. Archives départementales de la Gironde (ADG). Notaire Brigot, 3E2418.

Freixa, Adolfo

"Vizcaya en las rutas del mar," *Vida Vasca*, Vol. 26 (1947), pp. 194-95.

Gaffarel, Paul

Voyages des Français au Canada dans l'Amérique centrale et au Brésil dans les premières années du XVIe siècle. Imprimeries réunies, Lausanne, 1972.

Gallop, Rodney

A Book of the Basques. University of Nevada Press, Reno, 1930.

Gandia, Enrique de

Primitivos navegantes vascos. Ekin, Buenos Aires, 1942.

Garate, Justo

"Los Euskerianos tras los cetaceos," *Boletin de la real sociedad vascongada de los amigos del país*, Vol. 21 (1965), pp. 177-84.

Garcia de Cortazar y Ruiz de Aguirre, Jose Angel

Vizcaya en el siglo XV: aspectos económicos y sociales. Ediciones de la Caja de ahorros Viscaina, Bilbao, 1966.

Garcia de Palacio, Diego

Nautical Instruction, 1587. Terrenate Association, Bisbee, 1986.

Garcia-Frias, Juan

"El punto de la nave en la epoca anterior al cronometro," in *Anuario del instituto de estudios marítimos Juan de la Cosa*. Diputacion provincial de Santander, Santander, 1978, Vol. 2.

Garmendia Berasategui, Ignacio

Diccionario marítimo ilustrado. La Gran Enciclopedia Vasca, Bilbao, 1970.

Garmendia, P.

Trajes vascos del siglo XVI," *Revista internacional de estudios vascos*, No. 25 (1934), pp. 274-82, 521-24; No. 26 (1935), pp. 151-54; No. 27 (1936), pp. 126-33.

Gilchrist, John

"Exploration and Enterprise: the Newfoundland Fishery, c. 1497-1677," in *Canadian Business History*. MacMillan, Toronto, 1972.

Gordstidi, Angel

"Naves de Guipuzcoa en el siglo XVI," *Euskal Erria*, Vol. 55, No. 919, pp. 186-90.

Goyeneche, E.

'Bayonne et la région bayonnaise du XIIe au XVe siècle: étude d'histoire économique et sociale," Ph.D. thesis presented at l'École des chartes, 1949.

Graells, M.P.

Las ballenas en las costas oceanicas de España. Luis Aguado, Madrid, 1889.

Gray, E.

"The Atlantic or Biscay Whale, *balaena glacialis* and the Spitsbergen Whale Fishery of the seventeenth Century," *The Naturalist* (July 1937), pp. 153-56.

Grenier, Robert, and James A. Tuck

"Discovery in Labrador: a 16th-Century Basque Whaling Port and its Sunken Fleet," *National Geographic* (July 1985), pp. 40-71.

Guiard, Teófilo

Historia del consulado y casa de contratacion de Bilbao y del comercio de la villa. Biblioteca vascongada Villar, Bilbao, 1978.

——. "La villa de Bilbao," *Vida Vasca*, No. 20 (1943), pp. 233-48.

Habasque, Francisque

"Les traités de bonne correspondance entre le Labourd, la Biscaye et le Guipuzcoa," *Bulletin historique et philologique* (1894-95), pp. 560-74.

Hakluyt, Richard

The Principal Navigations, Voyages, Traffiques & Discoveries of the English nation, made by Sea or Over-land to the remote and farthest distant quarters of the Earth at any time within the compass of these 1600 yeeres. J. MacLehose & Sons, Glasgow 1903.

Hamilton, Earl J.

"Imports of American Gold and Silver into Spain, 1503-1660," *Quarterly Journal of Economics* (May 1929), pp. 436-72.

Harrisse, Henry

Découverte et évolution cartographique de Terre-Neuve. Welter, Paris, 1900.

Hawes, Charles B.

Whaling. W. Heinemann, London, 1924.

Heers, Jacques

Christophe Colomb. Hachette, Paris, 1981.

——. "Christophe Colomb le Génois," *L'Histoire*, No. 36 (July-Aug. 1981), pp. 76-85.

——. "Rivalité ou collaboration de la terre et de l'eau? position générale des problèmes," in *Travaux du Colloque international d'histoire maritime* (7th, Vienna 1665). S.E.V.P.E.N., Paris, 1965, pp. 13-63.

Hérubel, Marcel A.

"Baleines et baleiniers: étude d'économie maritime," *La Revue Maritime* (Ma 1930), pp. 591-633.

Hohman, E.P.

The American Whaleman: A Study of Life and Labour in the Whaling Industry. A gustin M. Kelley, Clifton, N.J., 1972.

Hoyarsabal, Martin de

Les voyages aventureux du capitaine Martin de Hoyarsabal, habitant de Cubiburu. Guillaume Millanges, Bordeaux, 1633.

Huarte, Angel de

"Las fábricas reales de Guipuzcoa," *Euskalerriaren Alde*, Vol. 17, No. 276, pp. 297-304 and 380-86.

Huxley, Selma

"Vascos en Terranova: dos cartas de afletamiento de naves en San Sebastián en 1564," *Boletin de estudios historicos sobre San Sebastián* (1978), pp. 191-200.

Ibabe, Enrique

Notas sobre la ceramica vasca. Aurman, Bilbao, 1980.

Iglesias, Felipe V.

"Los Guipuzcoanos en el mar," *Euskalerriaren Alde*, Vol. 16, No. 265, pp. 447-53.

Imaz, Jose Manuel

La industria pesquera en Guipuzcoa al final del siglo XVI. Excma, San Sebastián, 1944.

Innis, H.A.

"The Rise and Fall of the Spanish Fishery in Newfoundland," *Proceedings and Transactions of the Royal Society of Canada*, 3rd. Series, Vol. 25, section 11 (1931), pp. 51-70.

Institucion cultural de Cantabria

Annuario del instituto de estudios marítimos Juan de la Cosa. Diputacion provincial de Santander, Santander, 1978, Vol. 2.

Espizua, S. de

Los Vascos en America. Italica, Madrid, 1917.

Iturriza y Zabala, Juan Ramon de

Historia general de Vizcaya y epítome de las encartaciones. Arturo, Bilbao, 1967.

Izaguirre, Manuel

"El rescate del galeon vasco," *Viajar*, No. 70 (Jan. 1985), pp. 60-68.

Jenkins, James Travis

A History of the Whale Fisheries. H.F. & G. Witherby, London, 1921.

Juders, E.

Pesquerias españolas en los mares del Norte. No publisher, Madrid, 1901.

Labayen, Francisco M.

"Ferrerias y ferrones," *Vida Vasca*, No. 30 (1953), pp. 100-104.

——. "La pesca como medio de vida y su derivacion deportiva," *Vida Vasca*, No. 32 (1955), pp. 121-27.

Labayru y Goicoechea, Estanislo Jaime de

Historia general del Senorio de Vizcaya. La Gran Enciclopedia Vasca, Bilbao, 1899-1920.

Laborde, Jean

"La pêche de la baleine par les harponneurs basques," *Gure Herria*, Vol. 28, No. 5 (1951), pp. 257-69.

La Cepède

Histoire naturelle des cétacés. Year XIII of the Republic, Plassan, Paris, [1804].

Lafarga Lozano, Adolfo

Los Vascos en el descubrimiento y colonización de América. La Gran Enciclopedia Vasca, Bilbao, 1973.

La Jonkaire, A. de

Considérations sur la pêche de la baleine. No publisher, Paris, 1830.

Lander, R.L.
"An Assessment of the Numbers, Sizes and Types for English and Spanish Ships Mobilized for the Armada Campaign," *The Mariner's Mirror*, Vol. 63, No. 4 (Nov. 1977), pp. 359-69.

Lapeyre, H.
"Algunos datos sobre el movimiento del puerto de San Sebastián en tiempos de Felipe II," *Boletin de estudios historicos sobre San Sebastián* (1971), pp. 180-91.

La Roncière, Charles de
"La France arctique ou les baleiniers basques au Spitzberg," *Revue du Béarn et du Pays Basque* (1905), pp. 49-97.

Lasa, José I.
"Reales cedulas sobre las pesquerias de Terranova," *Aranzazu*, Vol. 57, Nos. 581 and 582, pp. 62-64 and 94-96.
——. "Vascos en Terranova y Labrador," *Aranzazu*, Vol. 55 (1975), pp. 21-24.

Laverdière, C.H. (ed.)
Oeuvres de Champlain. Université Laval, Québec, 1870, 3 vols.

Leizaola, Jesús Maria de
La Marina civil vasca en los siglos XIII, XIV y XV. Sendoa, San Sebastián, 1984.

Lery, Jean de
Histoire d'un voyage fait en la terre du Brésil. Bibliothèque romande, Lausanne, 1972.

Leslie, John
Narrative of Discovery and Adventure in the Polar Seas and Regions; with Illustrations of their Climate, Geology and Natural History; and an Account of the Whale-fishery. Oliver & Boyd, Edinburgh, 1835.

Lewis, M.
L'invincible Armada. Payot, Paris, 1962.

Lopez Piñeiro, José Maria

El arte de navegar en la España del Renacimiento. Labor, Barcelona, 1979.

Manzano Manzano, Juan

Colon y su secreto: el predescubrimiento. Cultura Hispanica, Madrid, 1982.

Marguet, F.

Histoire générale de la navigation du XVe au XXe siècle. Éditions géographiques, maritimes et coloniales, Paris, 1931.

Markham, Sir Clement

"On the Whale-Fisheries of the Basque Provinces of Spain," *Nature*, Vol. 25 (1882), pp. 365-68.

——. *Voyages of William Baffin*, 1612-1622. Hakluyt Society, London, 1881.

Martinez de Isasti, Lope

Compendio historical de la M.N. provincia de Guipuzcoa. I.R. Baroja, San Sebastián, 1850.

Medina, Pedro de

"Las cosas memorables que habia," *Euskalerriaren Alde*, Vol. 5, Nos. 97 and 98, pp. 544-46.

Meurgey, Jacques

"Saint-Jean-de-Luz et la pêche de la baleine au XVIIe siècle," *Bulletin de la Société des Sciences Lettres et Arts de Bayonne*, Vol. 45, Nos. 1 and 2, pp. 117-18.

Michel, F.

Le pays basque. Firmin Didot, Paris, 1857.

Michelena, Luis

"La grasa de pescado como medio de alumbrado," *Boletin de la real sociedad vascongada de los amigos del país*, Vol. 9 (1953), pp. 558-60.

Mitchell, Mairin

"Basque and British Seamen: some links in history," *Boletin de la real sociedad vascongada de los amigos del país*, Vol. 26 (1970), pp. 447-67.

Mollat, Michel

La vie quotidienne des gens de mer en Atlantique: IXe - XVIe siècle. Hachette, Paris, 1983.

——. *Histoire des pêches maritimes en France*. Bibliothèque historique Privat, Toulouse, 1987.

Moreno Echevarria, J.M.

"Los balleneros vascos," *Historia y Vida*, No. 138 (Sept. 1979), pp. 72-84.

Moussette, Marcel

"La pêche de la baleine; méthodes de capture de la baleine utilisées dans le golfe et l'estuaire du Saint-Laurent," *Revue d'histoire de la Gaspésie*, Vol. 10, No. 1 (Jan.-Mar. 1972), pp. 16-30.

Mugartegui, J.J. de

"Como se reclutaba el siglo XVI, en nuestras costas una tripulacion para la pesca del bacalao en Terra-Nova," *Revista internacional de los estudios vascos*, No. 19 (1928), pp. 632-36.

Musset, Lucien

"Quelques notes sur les baleiniers normands du Xe au XIIIe siècle," *Revue d'histoire économique et sociale*, Vol. 42, No. 2 (1964).

Noël, S.B.J.

Histoire générale des pêches anciennes et modernes. Imprimerie Royale, Paris, 1815.

Nogaret, J.

"Aperçus sur l'histoire de Saint-Jean-de-Luz depuis ses origines," *Bulletin de la Société des Sciences, Lettres et Arts de Bayonne* (1925), pp. 12-35.

——. "Petite histoire du pays basque français," *Bulletin de la Société des Sciences, Lettres et Arts de Bayonne*, Vol. 44, Nos. 1 and 2 (1923), pp. 5-95.

Oñativia, G. Hombrados

"En Canada y Groenlandia: el testimonio irrebatible de muchos nombres vascos," *Vida Vasca*, No. 57 (1980), n.p.

——. "Marinos vascos en el Canada," *Vida Vasca*, No. 52 (1975), n.p.

O'Shea

A. Navagero, Bayonne et le pays basque en 1528. No publisher, Bayonne, 1886.

Paré, Ambroise

Oeuvres complètes d'Ambroise Paré. J.B. Baillière, Paris, 1841.

Planté, Adrien

"Les Basques ont-ils une histoire?" in *La Tradition au pays basque*. Elkar, Donostia, 1982.

Pomey, Patrick

"Comment naviguait-on dans la Méditerrannée romaine?" *L'Histoire*, No. 36 (July-Aug. 1981), pp. 96-101.

Proulx, Jean-Pierre

Whaling in the North Atlantic From Earliest Times to the Mid-19th Century. Parks Canada, Ottawa, 1986.

Prowse, D.W.

A History of Newfoundland from the English Colonial and Foreign Records. Eyre & Spotiswoode, London, 1896.

Pulido Rubio, José

El piloto mayor de la casa de contratacion de Séville. Estudios hispano-americanos, Seville, 1950.

Purchas, S.
"Hakluyt Posthumus or Purchas His Pilgrimes," *Hakluyt Society*, Glasgow, 1906, Vols. 13 and 14.

Quinn, David B.
North American Discovery: circa 1000-1612. Harper & Row, New York, 1971.

Reade, John
"The Basques in North America," *Transactions and Proceedings of the Royal Society of Canada*, Vol. 6, section 2 (1888), pp. 21-39.

Rectoran, Pierre
Corsaires basques et bayonnais du XVe au XIXe siècle, pirates, flibustiers, boucaniers. E. Plumon, Bayonne, 1946.

Retana, J.M. Martin de
"Hollandeses, Ingleses y Norteamericanos aprendieron de los Vascos a cazar ballenas," *Vida Vasca*, No. 42 (1965), pp. 231.
——. "Los Vascos inventaron el ancla," *Vida Vasca*, No. 42 (1965), pp. 89-91.

Ricart y Giralt, José
"Salvamento de naufragos," *Boletin de la sociedad de Guipuzcoa*, Vol. 3 No. 10 (Jan. 1914), pp. 197-203; Vol. 4, No. 14 (Jan. 1915), pp. 32-39.

Ringer, James R.
"Progress report on the marine excavation of the Basque whaling vessel *San Juan* (1565): A Summary of the 1982 Field Season," *Research Bulletin*, No. 206 (Nov. 1983), Parks Canada, Ottawa.

Rodriguez, Angel
"La ceramica de Busturia," *Vida Vasca*, No. 20 (1943), p. 270-71.

Rohmer, Régis
Notes sur le commerce de Bayonne et les privilèges que lui accordèrent les rois d'Angleterre pendant la guerre de 100 ans. No publisher, Bayonne, 1913.

Ross, Lester A.

"Sixteenth-century Spanish Basque Coopering Technology: A Report on the Staved Containers Found in 1978-79 on the Wreck of the Whaling galleon *San Juan*, sunk in Red Bay, Labrador, AD 1565," Manuscript Report Series No. 408, Ottawa, Parks Canada, 1980.

Ruspoli, Mario

À la recherche du cachalot. Éditions de Paris, Paris, 1955.

Saint-Pierre, J.

"Le duel de Bayonne et du Labourd au XVIe siècle," *Gure Herria*, No. 5 (1950), pp. 193-200.

Salas, Javier de et F.G. Sola

Memoria sobre la industria y legislation de pesca. T. Fortanet, n.p., 1876.

Sanderson, Ivan T.

Follow the Whale. Little, Brown & Co., Boston, 1956.

Sañez Reguart, Antonio

Diccionario historico de las artes de la pesca nacional por el Comisario Real de Guerra y de Marina. Viuda de Joaquin de Iberra, Madrid, 1795, 5 vols.

Savary des Bruslons, Jacques

Dictionnaire universel de commerce, d'histoire naturelle et des arts et métiers. A.& Ant. Philibert, Copenhagen, 1759. 5 vols.

——. *Le parfait négociant ou instruction générale pour ce qui regarde le commerce* Frères Étienne, Paris, 1757.

Scammon, Charles M.

The Marine Mammals of the Northwestern Coast of North America Described and Illustrated, Together with an Account of the American Whale-fishery. Dover Publications, New York, 1968.

Scoresby, William

An Account of the Arctic Regions with a History and Description of the Northern Whale-fishery. Archibald Constable & Co., Edinburgh, 1820.

——. *The Arctic Regions and the Northern Whale-Fishery*. The Religious Tract Society, London, [183?].

Sée, Henri

"Le commerce en France au XVIe siècle," *Annales d'histoire économique et sociale*, No. 1 (1929), pp. 551-61.

Seoane y Ferrer, Ramon

Los marineros Guipuzcoanos. Revista general de marina, Madrid, 1908.

Slijper, E.J.

Whales. Hutchinson, London, 1962.

Soraluce, Pedro M. de

"El marinero euskaldun," *Euskal Erria*, Vol. 33, No. 554 (1895), pp. 468-72; No. 555 (1895), pp. 504-7; No. 556 (1895), pp. 521-25; No. 557 (1895), pp. 568-75; Vol. 34, No. 558 (1896), pp. 18-22.

Soraluce y Zubizarreta, Nicolas de

Historia general de Guipuzcoa. No publisher, Vitoria, 1870.

——. *Introducción, capítulo 1 y otras descripciones de la memoria acerca del origen y curso de las pescas y pesquerías de ballenas y de bacalaos asi que sobre el descubrimiento de los bancos et Isla de Terranova*. Hijos de Mantele, Vitoria, 1878.

Spain

Burgos. Archivo de la diputacion provincial. Fondo del consulado del mar y universidad de Mercaderes.

——. Madrid. Museo Naval. Coleccion Vargas Ponce.

——. Simancas. Archivo general (AGS). Guerra Antigua.

——. Valladolid. Archivo de la Real Chancilleria (ARC). Pleitos civiles.

Stevens, Willis

"Underwater Research at Red Bay, Labrador: A Summary of the 1981 Field Season," *Research Bulletin*, No. 194 (June 1983), Parks Canada, Ottawa.

Tellechea Idigoras, J. Ignacio

"El diezmo viejo de San Sebastián: 1511-1571," *Boletin de estudios historicos sobre San Sebastián* (1977), pp. 49-57.

The Basque Country

Tolosa. Archivo general de la diputacion de Guipuzcoa (AGDG). Corregimiento.

Oñate. Archivo historico de los protocolos de Guipuzcoa (AHPG). Partidos de Vergara, Azpeitia and San Sebastián.

Thomazi, A.

Histoire de la pêche des âges de pierre à nos jours. Payot, Paris, 1947.

Thurston, Harry

"The Basque Connections," *Equinox*, No. 12 (Nov.-Dec. 1983), pp. 46-59.

Touchard, Henri

"Les routes françaises de l'Atlantique jusqu'aux grandes découvertes," in *Travaux du Colloque international d'histoire maritime* (9th, Seville, 1967). S.E.V.P.E.N., Paris, 1969, pp. 357-75.

Trudel, François

"Les Inuit face à l'expansion commerciale européenne dans la région du détroit de Belle-Isle aux XVIe et XVIIe siècles," *Recherches amérindiennes au Québec*, Vol. 7, Nos. 3 and 4 (1978), pp. 49-58.

Tuck, James A.

"Excavations at Red Bay, Labrador," *Archaeology in Newfoundland and Labrador*, Historic Resources Division, Dept. of Culture, Recreation & Youth, Government of Newfoundland and Labrador, Annual Reports, No. 1 (1980), pp. 69-77; No. 2 (1981), pp. 68-87; No. 3 (1982), pp. 95-117; No. 4 (1983), pp. 70-81; No. 5 (1984), pp. 224-47, St. John's.

Tuck, James A., and R. Grenier

"A 16th-Century Basque Whaling Station in Labrador," *Scientific American*, Vol. 245, No. 5 (Nov. 1981), pp. 180-90.

Turgeon, Laurier

"Naufrages des terreneuviers bayonnais et luziens," *Société des Sciences, Lettres et Arts de Bayonne*, No. 134 (1978), pp. 1-9.

——. "Pêches basques en Atlantique Nord: XVIIe-XVIIIe siècle; étude d'économie maritime," Ph.D. thesis submitted to the Centre d'Études canadiennes de Bordeaux, 1982.

——. "Pêcheurs basques et Indiens des côtes du Québec au XVIe siècle," paper read at the *Colloque franco-québecois d'histoire rurale comparée*, held in Rochefort, July 5 to 8, 1982.

——. "Les pêches françaises à terreneuve d'après les archives notariales de Bordeaux: 1555-1614," paper read at the 11th congress of the *French Historical Society*, held in Quebec City, May 9 to 11, 1985.

Ugartechea y Salinas, J.M.

"La pesca tradicional en Lequeitio," *Anuario de Eusko-Folklore*, Vol. 22 (1967-68), pp. 9-155.

Usher, A.B.

"Spanish ships and shipping in the sixteenth and seventeenth centuries," in *Facts and Factors in Economic History*. Russell & Russell, New York, 1932.

Vaucaire, Michel

Histoire de la pêche de la baleine. Payot, Paris, 1941.

Veitia Linaje, Joseph

Norte de la contratación de las Indias occidentales. Juan Francisco de Blas, Séville, 1672. Reprinted: Ministerio de Hacienda, Madrid, 1981.

Velilla, I.A.

"La evolucion de la industria naviera en Bilbao," *Vida Vasca*, No. 15 (1938), pp. 123-27.

——. "Una vision de Bilbao en los siglos XV y XVI," *Vida Vasca*, No. 16 (1939), pp. 167.

Verdejo Iglesias, Felipe

"La Marina vasca: los guipuzcoanos en el mar," *Euskalerriaren Alde*, Vol. 16, No. 276 (1926), pp. 447-53.

Verlinden, Charles

Les origines de la civilisation atlantique de la Renaissance à l'Age des Lumières. Albin Michel, Paris, 1966.

Yturbide, Pierre

"La pêche des baleines au pays basque du XIIe au XVIIIe siècles," *Société bayonnaise d'études régionales*, supplemental bulletin No. 5 (1918), pp. 16-35.

——. "Les anciens traités de bonne correspondance entre les Basques de France et ceux d'Espagne," *Revista internacional de los estudios vascos*, No. 13 (1922), pp. 179-220.

Zabala, Alicia

Atalaya historica de la muy noble y muy leal villa de Bermeo. Juanta de Cultura de Vizcaya, Bilbao, 1964.

Zumalde, Iñaki

"Tras las huellas de los balleneros vascos en Terranova," *Deia*, Feb. 17, pp. 10; Feb. 24, pp. 4; March 2, pp. 4; March 9, pp. 4; March 23, pp. 4; March 30, pp. 6 (1980).